Reflections on the
Cuban Missile Crisis

RAYMOND L. GARTHOFF

Reflections on the
Cuban Missile Crisis

THE BROOKINGS INSTITUTION

Washington, D.C.

Library of Congress Cataloging-in-Publication data:

Garthoff, Raymond L.
Reflections on the Cuban missile crisis.
Includes index.
1. Cuban Missile Crisis, Oct. 1962.   I. Title.
E841.G37   1987   972.91′064   87-27824

ISBN 0-8157-3052-7
ISBN 0-8157-3051-9 (pbk.)

9 8 7 6 5 4 3 2 1

THE BROOKINGS INSTITUTION is an independent organization devoted to nonpartisan research, education, and publication in economics, government, foreign policy, and the social sciences generally. Its principal purposes are to aid in the development of sound public policies and to promote public understanding of issues of national importance.

The Institution was founded on December 8, 1927, to merge the activities of the Institute for Government Research, founded in 1916, the Institute of Economics, founded in 1922, and the Robert Brookings Graduate School of Economics and Government, founded in 1924.

The Board of Trustees is responsible for the general administration of the Institution, while the immediate direction of the policies, program, and staff is vested in the President, assisted by an advisory committee of the officers and staff. The by-laws of the Institution state: "It is the function of the Trustees to make possible the conduct of scientific research, and publication, under the most favorable conditions, and to safeguard the independence of the research staff in the pursuit of their studies and in the publication of the results of such studies. It is not a part of their function to determine, control, or influence the conduct of particular investigations or the conclusions reached."

The President bears final responsibility for the decision to publish a manuscript as a Brookings book. In reaching his judgment on the competence, accuracy, and objectivity of each study, the President is advised by the director of the appropriate research program and weighs the views of a panel of expert outside readers who report to him in confidence on the quality of the work. Publication of a work signifies that it is deemed a competent treatment worthy of public consideration but does not imply endorsement of conclusions or recommendations.

The Institution maintains its position of neutrality on issues of public policy in order to safeguard the intellectual freedom of the staff. Hence interpretations or conclusions in Brookings publications should be understood to be solely those of the authors and should not be attributed to the Institution, to its trustees, officers, or other staff members, or to the organizations that support its research.

Foreword

OVER THE twenty-five years since the Cuban missile crisis, much has been written about the crisis itself and the lessons that can be learned from it. Yet there remains much that has not been addressed, and even today new facts about the events and deliberations continue to emerge.

In this book Raymond L. Garthoff, a participant in the crisis deliberations in the U.S. government, reflects on the nature of the crisis, its consequences, and its lessons for the future. He presents a number of facts for the first time and provides a unique combination of memoir, historical analysis, and political interpretation. He gives particular attention to the aftermath and "afterlife" of the crisis and to its bearing on current and future policy.

The author also supplies a dimension of analysis usually neglected: the crisis as experienced by the Soviets, and the lessons they appear to have drawn from it. He emphasizes the need to include this integral element of the picture not only to broaden historical perspective, but particularly to understand the interaction of American and Soviet policymaking in the events leading up to the crisis, in the confrontation itself, and in the subsequent development of U.S.-Soviet relations.

Raymond Garthoff, now a senior fellow in the Brookings Foreign Policy Studies program, wishes to acknowledge his appreciation to many colleagues involved in the missile crisis, and other students of the episode, with whom he has on various occasions discussed aspects of the subject. He wishes also to express appreciation to the National Security Archive for making available its file of declassified documents. Finally, he wishes to thank Jeanette Morrison for editing the manuscript and Mark R. Thibault for verifying the published sources.

Brookings gratefully acknowledges the financial support for this book provided by the Andrew W. Mellon Foundation, the Carnegie Corporation of New York, and the John D. and Catherine T. MacArthur Foundation.

The views in this book are those of the author and should not be ascribed to the persons or foundations whose assistance is acknowledged, or to the trustees, officers, or other staff members of the Brookings Institution.

BRUCE K. MACLAURY
President

September 1987
Washington, D.C.

Contents

Purpose and Perspective

DO WE NEED more reflections on the Cuban missile crisis? The historical event itself was sufficiently important, and the twenty-fifth anniversary is a suitable occasion to redirect attention to the crisis and the lessons we can learn from it. I raise the question nonetheless because so much has already been written on the subject, including a spate of anniversary articles that have recently appeared and others yet to come. Moreover, the past decade has seen the declassification and release of numerous documents related to the crisis, again with more to come, and they complement—and in some cases modify—the picture of the Washington deliberations that has heretofore rested principally on the memoirs and reminiscences of a number of the key participants.

For perfectly natural reasons, commentary on the crisis in this country has focused almost entirely on *the American experience* of the event and the lessons we Americans have learned, or should learn, from it. In addition, the main reason so much attention has been given to the crisis is that it has rightly been regarded as the most intensive, dangerous, and climactic crisis of the cold war, and has thus become a unique historical source for the study of *crisis management*.

For various reasons, mainly the unsatisfactory outcome from the Soviet standpoint, the event has received much less attention in the Soviet Union, although in recent years there has been renewed interest. In the Soviet Union it is known as the "Caribbean crisis" rather than the "Cuban missile crisis"—a difference stemming from more than mere Soviet preference not to highlight the role of their missiles, as shall be shown. The paucity of Soviet

discussion has contributed to the relative American slighting of the
Soviet role, but it has not been the main cause. The primary reason
has been the intensity of the American decisionmaking experience,
above all to the participants, who have dominated the discussion
not only directly but also by providing the extensive record used
by political scientists and historians—a biasing factor compounded
by the release of extensive declassified documentary sources on
the American handling of the crisis.

Many events bearing on the unfolding of the crisis have not been
adequately taken into account in histories and analyses, and indeed
in some cases have not even been known. I shall provide new
information on a number of events affecting the course and outcome
of the crisis that have been neglected or unknown.

I was a participant in the missile crisis, as a staff-level adviser
in the State Department with experience in Soviet affairs, intelligence analysis, and politico-military affairs. While playing only a
supporting role in the crisis policymaking, I was privy to facts
about several developments during the crisis that have not heretofore been published, including information not known to more
senior participants who have written about the crisis.

In sum, the first aim of this study is to broaden the historical
analysis. A second is to supply both new information and a
somewhat different perspective, bringing in Soviet perceptions to
a larger extent than has been done. A third is to contribute to the
fund of memoir material, including a number of analytical and
action memoranda I wrote during the crisis, now declassified, that
are noted in the discussion and the texts of which are appended.
Finally, I shall discuss the direct and indirect consequences of the
Cuban missile crisis in the months and years following its resolution, also an important subject that has been given too little
attention.

One principal objective of this volume is to address the *interaction* of American and Soviet perceptions and actions in entering
the crisis, and in resolving it. The lack of appreciation of such
interaction will become apparent in later discussions of the differing
retrospective evaluations of the crisis and lessons drawn from it by
the two sides. The very title of this study—and all other American

accounts—draws attention to an important difference in Soviet and American perceptions and perspectives. Any reference to this subject in the United States is routinely to the "Cuban missile crisis" of October 1962. The crisis is often seen as having lasted thirteen days (October 16–28), from the time Washington discovered construction was under way in Cuba on launch facilities for Soviet medium-range missiles, to the day Chairman of the Council of Ministers Nikita S. Khrushchev formally agreed to withdraw missiles from Cuba and President John F. Kennedy pledged not to invade that country. Fuller accounts also include the period from October 28 to November 20, when intensive negotiations more completely spelled out and modified the settlement that had been reached, the U.S. naval quarantine was lifted, and the special alert status of the military forces of the two countries ended.

Soviet accounts of the "Caribbean crisis" emphasize the persisting American hostility to Castro's rule in Cuba, the failure of the Bay of Pigs invasion by American-armed Cuban emigrés in April 1961, and an alleged continuing American threat to invade Cuba. The more immediate crisis itself is seen as beginning, not on October 16, but on October 22, with President Kennedy's announcement that the Soviet Union was installing medium-range missiles in Cuba and his demand that they be removed, accompanied by a naval quarantine to prevent any further shipment of offensive arms to Cuba. That marked the beginning of an intensive six days of deliberation in Moscow. The resolution of the crisis in principle on October 28 is stressed, with little attention to the subsequent three weeks of negotiation before it was in fact settled.

Several things should be said about the underlying differences in perspective. First, contrary to claims often made in both countries, neither holds a monopoly on the truth. Both have some legitimate basis for attributing different values to different facts, and even to the same facts. The facts themselves, of course, however well known, interpreted, or ignored, are the same for both.

Another point I would make about the difference in perspective is that even today the crisis is not sufficiently understood. Analysts on both sides have focused on how the experience of the crisis has made successive leaders more prudent and more sharply aware of the need to avoid actions that could bring us again to the brink of war. But there is inadequate understanding in the United States as to why that event is called the "Caribbean crisis" in the Soviet Union, and how it could be seriously regarded as stemming even in part from *American* actions. There is inadequate understanding in the Soviet Union as to why it is properly thought of in the United States as a crisis brought about by the secret introduction of *Soviet* missiles into Cuba. And in both countries there is insufficient attention to and understanding of the whole process of interaction, involving not only differing perspectives but differing frameworks of relevant reality—or different sets of facts. Very different base levels of openness on source material in the two countries compound the problem of trying to achieve some sort of integrated political and historical perspective.

To broaden the context of the analysis, I categorize the crisis in terms of six stages: (1) the developments before October 16, 1962, including the Soviet decision in the late spring to deploy medium-range missiles in Cuba; (2) October 16–22, the period of intense secret internal deliberation and decision within the U.S. government; (3) October 22–28, the superpower confrontation and negotiation climaxing in an agreement basically resolving the crisis; (4) October 28–November 20, the clarification, implementation, and also modification of the basic agreement, including crucial Soviet-Cuban negotiation over some issues; (5) the aftermath of the crisis, in particular the impact on U.S.-Soviet relations for the year until the assassination of President Kennedy on November 22, 1963; and (6) the "afterlife" or resurrection of the issue of possible Soviet offensive arms in Cuba, other than missiles, that arose on several occasions in the 1970s. Finally, I turn to the long-term legacy of the crisis, its importance in its own right, and the light it sheds in retrospectively evaluating the crisis itself and drawing lessons from it.

The Soviet Decision

SOVIET ACCOUNTS of the "Caribbean crisis" stress many indications that after the failure of the Bay of Pigs invasion in April 1961, the leaders of the United States continued to seek ways to remove Fidel Castro and communism from Cuba. That is generally true. Most Soviet accounts, however, while more or less correctly noting various U.S. political, covert, and military actions in 1961–62, incorrectly conclude from that evidence that there was a policy and firm plan for a new invasion of Cuba by the United States' armed forces.[1] No doubt a military contingency "plan" was on file (the United States in 1941 even had a "war plan" for conflict with Great Britain), but there was no political decision or intention to invade Cuba before October 1962.

Nonetheless, it has since been revealed on the basis of congressional investigations and declassification of secret documents that the Kennedy administration was responsible after November 30, 1961, for sending sabotage and diversionary units of Cuban emigrés on raids into Cuba (under a covert action plan called "Operation Mongoose") and even for plotting to kill Castro.

It was not unreasonable for Castro and the Soviet government to be concerned over the possibility of intensified U.S. hostile action against Cuba in 1962.

---

1. I. D. Statsenko, "On Some Military-Political Aspects of the Caribbean Crisis," *Latinskaya Amerika* (Latin America), no. 6 (November–December 1977), pp. 108–17. Major General Igor D. Statsenko was one of the senior commanders of Soviet forces in Cuba in 1962. At that time, he had been freshly promoted to one-star general officer rank and was only forty-five years old. Some years later he was retired into the reserve with the same rank.

According to Nikita Khrushchev's unofficial but authenticated memoir (published in two volumes, in 1970 and 1974, in the United States under the title *Khrushchev Remembers*)[2], he first thought of stationing Soviet long-range missiles in Cuba in May 1962: "We were sure that the Americans would never reconcile themselves to the existence of Castro's Cuba. They feared, as much as we hoped, that a Socialist Cuba might become a magnet that would attract other Latin American countries to Socialism. . . . It was clear to me that we might very well lose Cuba if we didn't take some decisive steps in her defense. . . . It was during my visit to Bulgaria [May 14–20, 1962] that I had the idea of installing missiles with nuclear warheads in Cuba without letting the United States find out they were there until it was too late to do anything about them." Khrushchev stated, as he had officially in December 1962 to the Supreme Soviet after the crisis, that the rationale for the missiles was to deter an American invasion of Cuba. "The main thing was that the installation of our missiles in Cuba would, I thought, restrain the United States from precipitous military action against Castro's Government." But in his memoirs he added an important point not made in the official Soviet statements in 1962 or in later Soviet commentaries: "In addition to protecting Cuba, our missiles would have equalized what the West likes to call 'the balance of power'." And he went on to spotlight a psychological-political consideration: "The Americans had surrounded our country with military bases and threatened us with nuclear weapons, and now they would learn just what it feels like to have enemy missiles pointing at you; we'd be doing nothing more than giving them a little of their own medicine."[3]

We do know, from contemporary reporting in *Pravda*, that while in Bulgaria Khrushchev strongly criticized the installation of

2. Strobe Talbott, ed. and trans., *Khrushchev Remembers*, 2 vols. (Boston: Little, Brown, 1970, 1974). The authenticity of the taped Khrushchev memoirs was initially subject to skepticism in scholarly circles, but expert analysis comparing the voice prints with recorded Khrushchev statements established beyond doubt the authenticity of the memoirs. He may not, of course, have told the whole truth, or even remembered everything accurately, but his memoirs remain a very useful source.

3. Talbott, ed. and trans., *Khrushchev Remembers* (1970), pp. 492–94.

American intermediate-range missiles in Turkey.[4] A few days later he also criticized a statement by President Kennedy that the United States might under certain circumstances be the first to resort to nuclear weapons, an assertion the Soviets interpreted as representing American rhetoric supporting coercive use of its strategic nuclear superiority.[5]

Khrushchev's claim that the idea was his own has not been established; most, but not all, American analysts believe it likely (as do I). Castro has, on different occasions, made contradictory statements as to whether the initiative was Soviet or Cuban. The most plausible account by Castro was given in an interview with *Le Monde* several months after the crisis, in which he stated that the Soviets proposed stationing the missiles in Cuba "to strengthen the socialist camp on the world scale." He then added: "Since we were already receiving a large amount of assistance from the socialist camp, we decided that we could not refuse. That is why we accepted them. It was not in order to ensure our own defense, but primarily to strengthen socialism on the international scale."[6] He made the same points publicly in 1965, after Khrushchev's ouster, declaring that the Soviets had proposed the missile deployment, and despite the "risk," he had accepted the missiles "for the sake of strengthening the socialist camp"; this speech was published in *Pravda*.[7] Castro has attributed the idea to the Soviets on several other occasions as well.[8]

Precisely when the decision was made is also not known, but it

4. "Celebration of Fraternal Friendship on Bulgarian Soil, Speech by Comrade N. S. Khrushchev," *Pravda*, May 17, 1962.

5. "Rally of 250,000 Working People in Sofia in Honor of Soviet Party-Government Delegation, Speech by Comrade N. S. Khrushchev," *Pravda*, May 20, 1962.

6. Claude Julien, interview with Castro, "Kennedy-Castro," *Le Monde*, March 22, 1963.

7. "The Struggle against Imperialism Demands Unity and Solidarity of Revolutionary Forces, Speech by Fidel Castro at a Meeting at the University of Havana," *Pravda*, March 18, 1965.

8. For example, see Tad Szulc, "Castro on John Kennedy and the Missile Crisis," *Los Angeles Times*, April 15, 1984, an article based on an interview with Castro.

was probably in May or June, possibly slightly earlier or later.[9] (It could not have been much later given logistical and operational considerations.) The visit of Cuban Defense Minister Raul Castro to Moscow in early July may well have been in part related, although that visit could simply have involved consultations on the flow of other Soviet arms that were being sent to Cuba in large quantities by the mid-summer of 1962.

In his memoirs Khrushchev emphasized that the Soviet decision was, "from the outset, worked out in the collective leadership. It wasn't until after two or three lengthy discussions of the matter that we decided it was worth the risk to install missiles on Cuba in the first place." That statement is probably true, although to date nothing in the published Soviet literature bears directly on the leadership decision to place missiles in Cuba. Khrushchev also said: "I had wanted my comrades [in the Party Presidium] to accept and support the decision with a clear conscience and a full understanding of what the consequences of putting the missiles on Cuba might be—namely, war with the United States."[10] I find that assertion unconvincing. Khrushchev in retrospect may have wished to recall that the risks of a serious crisis were foreseen, weighed, and accepted. Perhaps. But I, for one, doubt it. Certainly he did, however, want to ensure collective responsibility for the decision.

Again, there is nothing in the published Soviet literature, nor do we in the West have any other reliable source of information, about the calculations of the Soviet leadership in making this decision.[11]

9. Soviet-Cuban relations had been troubled in the first months of 1962, although even then the leaders of both countries probably wished to improve them. In March Castro had purged from the leadership an orthodox and Soviet-trained Communist party leader, Aníbal Escalante. Military shipments from the Soviets for the first half of 1962 were reduced. Cuban interest in joining the Warsaw Pact was rebuffed. But from June on, relations visibly improved. Military aid grew enormously. Contacts increased on a wide range of subjects. And speeches by Castro and other Cuban leaders showed a new confidence.

10. Talbott, ed. and trans., *Khrushchev Remembers* (1970), pp. 498–99.

11. Former Soviet diplomat Arkady Shevchenko, who defected in 1978, has described the reactions of some Soviet officials to the crisis. In 1962 he was in the Soviet delegation to the Committee on Disarmament in Geneva, and he states that the Soviet mission there received no instructions or information throughout the crisis. Later, in Moscow, he heard that the idea of sending the missiles to

Obviously it was decided to install the missiles, and to do so in secrecy. The decision to undertake the action in secrecy, rather than publicly announcing it in advance, had a more significant effect on the American reaction and the whole course of events than may have been appreciated in Moscow at the time, or even in retrospect.

While inquiries continue into the Soviet motivation for placing missiles in Cuba,[12] there is a general consensus that the principal motivation was to redress the publicly revealed serious imbalance in the strategic nuclear balance.[13] No other explanation satisfactorily accounts for the action. Uncertainties remain as to whether Khrushchev would have overplayed his hand in attempting to use a suddenly disclosed new position of strength to buttress, for example, renewed demands on Berlin, or for some other objective. No doubt the Soviet leaders hoped and even expected that such a dramatic increment to their strategic military power would have political and military dividends for an activist Soviet foreign policy. But the strongest motive that would have led to a consensus among the Soviet leaders on taking a risk in the Cuban missile venture was almost certainly a perceived need to prevent the United States from using its growing strategic superiority to compel Soviet concessions on various issues under contention. Forty Soviet medium- and intermediate-range missile launchers in Cuba, while

---

Cuba was Khrushchev's and not that of the Soviet military (or the Cubans), and that there were no contingency plans on how to react to American advance discovery and demand for the withdrawal of the missiles. He also doubts that Anatoly Dobrynin or even Andrei Gromyko knew about the missiles before the crisis. All of that is quite plausible, indeed likely, but Shevchenko's second- and third-hand account is of little corroborative value. See Arkady N. Shevchenko, *Breaking with Moscow* (New York: Alfred A. Knopf, 1985), pp. 115–19, 154, 198.

12. The most current is an article by Richard Ned Lebow, "Khrushchev and the Cuban Missile Crisis," forthcoming.

13. There is no need here to recapitulate the many articles dealing with this subject. One of the first and best is Arnold L. Horelick, "The Cuban Missile Crisis: An Analysis of Soviet Calculations and Behavior," *World Politics,* vol. 16 (April 1964), pp. 363–89. There is also extensive discussion of Soviet motivations and actions in the most comprehensive overall analysis of the crisis, Graham T. Allison, *Essence of Decision: Explaining the Cuban Missile Crisis* (Boston: Little, Brown, 1971), esp. pp. 40–56, 102–17.

in no way conferring a decisive strategic advantage that would free Soviet hands, could be expected to help restrain American actions until the Soviet Union fielded enough intercontinental ballistic missiles to provide a more reliable deterrent.

Khrushchev personally had earlier been largely responsible for an exaggeration of the image of Soviet strategic power. This fact no doubt increased his personal stake in recovering Soviet standing. But it was the shared judgment of the leadership that world political perceptions of the strategic balance mattered, and that the Soviet Union's position in 1962 needed shoring up, that led to the decision.

The explanation for the deployment subsequently given by the Soviets—to deter an American attack on Cuba—was not only convenient but virtually necessary once the crisis had been resolved by withdrawing the missiles in exchange for an American pledge not to attack Cuba. But it was a supplementary and secondary reason for the decision.

The idea that Khrushchev saw the deployment as a test of Kennedy's will, or as feasible because of a misjudgment of Kennedy's will (after the Bay of Pigs and their summit encounter at Vienna in 1961), has been fairly well debunked,[14] although it was prominent in explanations of Soviet action among White House advisers during and after the 1962 crisis. Moreover, while Soviet miscalculation of the U.S. reaction clearly occurred, judgments on this matter may have facilitated the decision but would not have been its purpose.

Similarly, the idea that the Soviet leaders intended from the outset to trade the missiles in Cuba for U.S. missiles in Turkey is not credible. This was strictly an ad hoc objective born of the crisis confrontation, and even then not made the central element of a compromise.

No official Soviet commentaries since the crisis have acknowledged that the principal motivation for the decision to install the missiles in Cuba was to bolster Soviet strategic military power.

14. In particular, see Richard Ned Lebow, "The Cuban Missile Crisis: Reading the Lessons Correctly," *Political Science Quarterly,* vol. 98 (Fall 1983), pp. 447–78; and Lebow, "Deterrence Failure Revisited," *International Security,* vol. 12 (Summer 1987), pp. 197–213.

This would require admitting not only that Soviet strategic power needed reinforcement in 1962, but that the Soviets had failed in the attempt and been compelled to settle for a lesser concession in the compromise settlement. The argument that the missiles were to deter invasion of Cuba logically accounts for the decision to remove them when the United States pledged not to attack; an admission that they were needed to support broader Soviet political-military standing would not justify their removal even if Cuban security was assured.

Khrushchev, though avowing the official argument, came close to such an admission in his earlier-cited unofficial and unauthorized memoir. Castro has admitted it in his statements that the step was justified to him by the Soviets as one needed to strengthen the socialist camp in the global correlation of forces. There is a third witness: First Deputy Prime Minister and veteran Politburo member Anastas Mikoyan.

On November 30, 1962, on his way back to Moscow from important negotiations with Castro in Havana, Mikoyan spoke to the Warsaw Pact ambassadors in Washington. Mindful that the Soviet Union had not consulted with its Pact allies either on the decision to place the missiles in Cuba or on the decision to remove them, he explained that the missiles had been intended both to defend socialist Cuba, the official explanation, *and* to achieve a shift in the balance of power between the socialist and capitalist worlds. Mikoyan also told the ambassadors frankly that (in the recollection of one present) "after evaluating the strong American reaction during the crisis, however, the Presidium had decided against risking the security of the Soviet Union and its allies for the sake of Cuba." This account is by the then Hungarian chargé d'affaires, János Radványi, who later defected.[15]

In deciding to install the missiles secretly, the Soviet leaders failed to understand that while they had a good case for contending that their action was legal and comparable to the U.S. actions in

15. See János Radványi, *Hungary and the Superpowers: The 1956 Revolution and Realpolitik* (Stanford: Hoover Institution Press, 1972), p. 137. Radványi's account rings true, and he has been a reliable source on other developments he experienced firsthand.

establishing bases near the Soviet Union, their use of secrecy and deception would undercut the rationale of normalcy and legitimacy. If it was all above board, why do it surreptitiously? That was *not* comparable to what the United States had done. Of course, one can appreciate their belief that a sudden fait accompli would maximize the impact, but they did not adequately recognize the risks of premature American discovery and the adverse impact on their position of a sudden *American* announcement of the secret Soviet activity. I have recently asked a number of the 1962 policymakers what they think the American position would have been if the Soviet Union and Cuba had announced plans for a limited deployment of Soviet missiles in Cuba (the forty launchers planned, for example, were not discrepant from the forty-five launchers the United States had deployed in Italy and Turkey). All believed it was much less likely that the U.S. government would have sought, or been able, to compel retraction of the Soviet decision and preclude deployment.

The Soviet leaders also no doubt persuaded themselves much more effectively than they did the Americans that defensive intent meant the missiles were not really "offensive." There is a tendency on each side to see one's own weapons of all kinds as not being offensive, while regarding even tactically or strategically defensive weaponry of the adversary as contributing to a threat. But by carrying this argument to the point of giving misleading and even false assurances to the American leadership, the Soviets only ensured American attribution of a more hostile intent to themselves. The Soviet leadership was also undoubtedly moved by familiar psychological factors such as self-assurance of success and banishment from their thinking of the prospect or consequences of failure.

On September 17, at a time when Khrushchev and his colleagues must have been considering the possible American reactions to their missile deployment in the light of cautionary statements made by President Kennedy on September 4 and 13 (discussed below), Khrushchev took the occasion of a visit by Austrian Vice Chancellor Bruno Pittermann to try preemptively to deter an American blockade. There were, at the time, a number of calls by American political figures outside the administration for a blockade to put pressure on Cuba, and the subject was a natural one for Khrushchev to comment on without reference to the secret missile deployment under way. But Khrushchev undoubtedly expected the Austrians to pass along to the Americans his statement on the issue, so he saw it as an opportunity to influence the thinking of the American leadership. He told Pittermann that the United States intended to blockade Cuba, and that a blockade was an act of war. The Soviet government, he said, had instructed Soviet ships to proceed despite any interference by American warships, and if necessary such attempts at interference would be met by Soviet military means. This was, as events were later to demonstrate, a bluff. Moreover, it became clear in October that while long aware of the possibility of an American blockade, the Soviet leaders had not seriously considered how to meet one.

On October 15, on the very eve of the crisis, when the Soviet attempt to install the missiles surreptitiously seemed likely to succeed, Khrushchev told another visitor, Finnish President Urho Kekkonen, that he "now" believed that the United States would not attack Cuba. This statement may not have been intended as a signal to the United States.

The next day, October 16, Khrushchev had a long conversation with the new American ambassador, Foy D. Kohler. Three items in the discussion were, in retrospect, indirectly relevant to the crisis soon to unfold. First, Cuba came up in terms of an assurance by Khrushchev that a planned fishing port at Mariel, which Cuba had announced the Soviet Union would help it build, would be entirely nonmilitary. This response to an American query may have been intended to lull broader American concerns about Soviet military activities in Cuba, but it was itself true. Second, Kohler expressed U.S. regret over the accidental intrusion of a U-2 high-flying reconnaissance aircraft into Soviet airspace over Sakhalin Island on August 30, an action the Soviets had protested. And finally, Khrushchev sharply objected to the American placement of Jupiter intermediate-range ballistic missiles in Turkey and Italy.[16]

16. Kohler's detailed report of his long discussion with Khrushchev was dispatched to Washington in a series of cables. One cable, reporting the Cuban

By early September 1962 rumors and reports in the American press of Soviet missiles in Cuba were increasing. In addition, in March the U.S. government had established a combined CIA-military center at Opa-Locka base near Miami, Florida, to interview the steady stream of Cubans emigrating to the United States. This intelligence collection center received hundreds of reports of sightings of missiles. Many of these were sightings of surface-to-air missiles, which the Soviets began to deploy at the end of August; many were not missiles at all. (Similar reports had begun to be received as early as 1960, before Cuba and the Soviet Union had even established diplomatic relations.) In retrospect, at least one report of a missile sighting on September 12 was almost certainly of a Soviet SS-4 medium-range missile—but at the time it could not be confirmed, and hundreds of other reports were in error or unsubstantiated.[17] The same was true of reports from other sources. Nonetheless the administration came under increasing pressure. On August 31 Senator Kenneth Keating, a Republican from New York, began a steady campaign claiming that there were Soviet offensive missiles in Cuba and that the Kennedy administration was covering up this fact.[18]

By early September the Soviets opened a deliberate campaign

---

fishing port and U-2 exchanges, has been declassified; other cables in a series reporting on the discussion, including the one dealing with the Jupiters in Turkey and Italy, have apparently not yet been declassified.

The reason that Khrushchev would have had the Jupiters in Turkey on his mind will be discussed later; briefly, they were just reaching full operational status.

17. The CIA chief of the collection center in 1962 has written an interesting account that stresses this report but seriously overstates its impact in Washington. See Justin F. Gleichauf, "Red Presence in Cuba: The Genesis of a Crisis," *Army*, vol. 29 (November 1979), pp. 34–38.

Two other reports were, in retrospect, also possibly SS-4s; none of the others is believed to have been.

18. Senator Keating steadfastly refused to divulge the sources of his information, even when pointedly asked by a fellow conservative Republican, CIA Director John McCone. Some of his information, accurate and not, was evidently leaked by one or more disgruntled activists in U.S. intelligence organizations. Some, not even available in U.S. official hands, probably came from a certain Western ambassador in Havana whose capital had shown no interest in his alarmist reports home.

to counter any American suspicions. On September 4, Soviet Ambassador to the U.S. Anatoly Dobrynin told Attorney General Robert Kennedy that Khrushchev had sent his assurance that the Soviet government would not make any trouble—for example, over Berlin—for the president before the impending American congressional elections. Two days later Dobrynin met with White House aide Theodore Sorensen and passed on another message to the president, that Khrushchev might visit the United Nations in the second half of November (that is, after the U.S. elections), thus hinting at the possible opportunity for a meeting, as well as again implying that there would be no challenges in the meantime. And the day after that, he met with U.S. Ambassador to the UN Adlai Stevenson in New York and reassured him that only defensive weapons were being supplied to Cuba. Dobrynin had been instructed to give these assurances. He had *not,* moreover, been informed by Moscow that missiles were being deployed.[19]

On September 4 President Kennedy issued a public statement that there was no evidence of "offensive ground-to-ground missiles," or of "other significant offensive capability" in Cuba, but he pointedly added: "Were it to be otherwise, the gravest issues would arise."[20] On September 11, TASS carried a statement authorized by the Soviet government that seemed to deny that there were or would be offensive arms in Cuba; it said: "The arms and military equipment sent to Cuba are designated solely for defensive purposes," and also that "there is no need for the Soviet Union to shift its weapons for the repulse of aggression, for a retaliatory strike, to any other country, for instance Cuba. . . . There is no need to search for sites for them beyond the boundaries

19. Informed Soviet diplomatic sources have privately confirmed to me that Dobrynin was not told about the missiles until after the crisis broke.

20. "U.S. Reaffirms Policy on Prevention of Aggressive Actions by Cuba: Statement by President Kennedy," September 4, 1962, *Department of State Bulletin,* vol. 47 (September 24, 1962), p. 450. (Hereafter *State Bulletin.*)

Kennedy's statement was prompted by concern over both the public debate in the United States and, significantly, by skepticism over Dobrynin's assurance to Robert Kennedy earlier that same day. See Robert F. Kennedy, *Thirteen Days: A Memoir of the Cuban Missile Crisis* (New York: W. W. Norton, 1969), pp. 25–27.

of the Soviet Union."[21] The clear, and intended, impression was
that Soviet strategic missiles would not be sent to Cuba. On
September 13 Kennedy again made a public statement denying the
presence of offensive missiles in Cuba, stressing the distinction
from defensive arms, and seeking to sharpen the warning. He said
that if Cuba should ever "become an offensive military base of
significant capacity for the Soviet Union, then this country will do
whatever must be done to protect its own security and that of its
allies."[22]

Most American analyses of the crisis have not considered
relevant another range of contemporaneous developments, although these events were especially noted in Moscow and Havana.
On August 24, the anti-Castro Cuban emigré organization Alpha
66 launched a daring speedboat strafing attack on a Cuban seaside
hotel near Havana where Soviet military technicians were known
to congregate, killing a score of Russians and Cubans. Although
this particular raid was apparently not sanctioned by the United
States, the Cuban exile organization responsible was permitted to
base itself in Florida. On September 10 the same group attacked a
British and two Cuban cargo ships just north of Cuba. Again on
October 7 Alpha 66 carried out another raid against the island.

On September 5 Secretary of State Dean Rusk told nineteen
Latin American ambassadors in Washington that the United States
would work to prevent the spread of communism in the Western
Hemisphere. On September 8 Cuban exile leaders in the United
States publicly called on the Kennedy administration to support
resumption of large-scale subversive activities to bring down the
Castro regime. Between September 14 and 18 former Vice-Presi-
dent Richard Nixon and Senators Barry Goldwater, Strom Thur-
mond, John Tower, Hugh Scott, and Keating all called for a
blockade of Cuba to end any Soviet military assistance (and even

21. "TASS Statement," September 11, 1962, *Vneshnyaya politika Sovetskogo
Soyuza i mezhdunarodnyye otnosheniya, sbornik dokumentov, 1962 god* (The
Foreign Policy of the Soviet Union and International Relations, A Collection of
Documents, 1962) (Moscow: Institute of International Relations [IMO], 1963),
pp. 356–57. (Hereafter *Vneshnyaya politika, 1962.*)

22. "The President's News Conference of September 13, 1962," *Public Papers
of the Presidents: John F. Kennedy, 1962* (Government Printing Office, 1963), p.
674. (Hereafter *Public Papers: Kennedy, 1962.*)

liberal Senator Jacob Javits asked the president to demand an end to Soviet military assistance and take whatever action was necessary). On September 26 Congress passed a resolution sanctioning the use of force, if necessary, to restrain Cuban aggression and subversion in the Western Hemisphere. On October 3 President Kennedy signed it. That same day twenty Latin American foreign ministers issued a statement in Washington condemning any attempt to make Cuba an armed base for communist penetration of the Americas. On October 8 the U.S. Congress acted to withhold aid from any country that traded with Cuba (a move that evoked protests from such allies and neutrals as Great Britain and Sweden).

One development in this period, not (presumably) known to the Soviet leaders, nor for that matter to most American leaders, was a series of continuing meetings of the secret Special Group (Augmented) that had been established in November 1961 to conduct covert operations against Cuba under the code-name "Mongoose." Attorney General Kennedy was a driving force in this covert action program. A Washington headquarters group had been set up under Major General Edward Lansdale and a CIA "Task Force W" in Florida under William K. Harvey, both veteran covert action managers. The operation came to involve 400 Americans, about 2,000 Cubans, a private navy of fast boats, and an annual budget of about $50 million. Task Force W carried out a wide range of activities, initially mostly against Cuban ships and aircraft outside Cuba (and non-Cuban ships engaged in the Cuba trade), such as contaminating sugar shipments out of Cuba and tampering with industrial imports into the country. A new phase, calling for more raids into Cuba, opened in September.[23] On September 27 a CIA sabotage team in Cuba was arrested.

23. See *Alleged Assassination Plots Involving Foreign Leaders,* An Interim Report of the Senate Select Committee to Study Governmental Operations with Respect to Intelligence Activities, S. Rept. 94-465, 94 Cong. 1 sess. (GPO, 1975), pp. 139–43; John Prados, *Presidents' Secret Wars: CIA and Pentagon Secret Operations since World War II* (New York: William Morrow, 1986), pp. 210–13; and Arthur M. Schlesinger, Jr., *Robert Kennedy and His Times* (Boston: Houghton Mifflin, 1978), pp. 477–80.

A Miami CIA station was also established, in probable violation of the law banning CIA operations in the United States, to say nothing of organizing activities that contravened the Neutrality Act. It was headed by Theodore G.

On October 4, a meeting of the Special Group (Augmented) saw an argument between CIA Director John A. McCone and Robert Kennedy over why the program was going so slowly, which led to a decision to step up operations including the dispatch of sabotage teams into Cuba. At least three meetings followed, including one on October 16 in between the two meetings in the White House that day on the missiles in Cuba.[24] With the advent of the missile crisis the attention of all the U.S. government leaders shifted to that event, although covert operations were not forgotten.[25]

On October 12 a State Department spokesman said that although the United States did not "sanction" emigré raids on Cuba, it was not prepared to act against the Cuban emigrés who undertook them, and warned that foreign shippers who traded with Cuba took a risk.

President Kennedy believed that in his two September statements he had made a clear and strong warning to the Soviet leaders, although he was also attempting to reassure the American people and refute those who were claiming that a Soviet offensive missile threat already existed in Cuba.

Theodore Sorensen was very close to the president and drafted his September statements and most public statements on the Cuban situation and his personal messages to Khrushchev. Even more important, he was able to gauge President Kennedy's thinking unusually well. In a conference of veterans of the missile crisis and

---

Shackley and Thomas G. Clines, both later to become better known for questionable unofficial covert activities after their retirement.

24. Central Intelligence Agency, "Memorandum of Mongoose Meeting Held on Thursday, October 4, 1962" (now declassified), cited in Prados, *Presidents' Secret Wars,* p. 213. See also *Alleged Assassination Plots,* S. Rept. 94-465, p. 147.

25. Robert A. Hurwitch, State Department coordinator of Cuban affairs, proposed in the first days of crisis deliberations that one solution to the missile problem might be to send Cuban exiles in unmarked aircraft to bomb the missile sites, with a cover story that they were targeting oil refineries. Whatever appeal there might have been for removing in a surreptitious way missiles that had been surreptitiously brought in was overcome by doubts as to the proposal's effectiveness and the memory of the Bay of Pigs. Secretary Rusk turned the idea down flat, and it did not go beyond him. See Robert A. Hurwitch, "The Cuban Missile Crisis," *Foreign Service Journal,* vol. 48 (July 1971), pp. 17–20.

scholars studying it, in March 1987, Sorensen made a revealing statement. With regard to Kennedy's September statements in effect saying the United States would accept the large Soviet military assistance to Cuba then under way but would not accept strategic offensive missiles, Sorensen stated his belief that the president had "drawn the line" at what he thought the Soviets would not do. Everyone except McCone had agreed that the Soviets would not put offensive missiles in Cuba. Kennedy meant to draw a line that would preclude a serious change in the strategic balance, but believed *no* missiles was a safe place to draw it. Sorensen believes "the President drew the line precisely where he thought the Soviets were not and would not be; that is to say, if we had known that the Soviets were putting 40 missiles in Cuba, we might under this hypothesis have drawn the line at 100, and said with great fanfare that we would absolutely not tolerate the presence of more than 100 missiles in Cuba."[26]

On October 3 Undersecretary of State George W. Ball testified to Congress that "our intelligence is very good" that the military equipment supplied to Cuba "does not offer any offensive capabilities."[27] And on October 14, McGeorge Bundy, national security adviser to the president, stated on national television: "I *know* that there is no present evidence, and I think that there is no present likelihood that the Cubans and the Cuban Government and the Soviet Government would in combination attempt to install a major offensive capability."[28]

Meanwhile, the first Soviet medium-range missile equipment had arrived in Cuba in the large-hatch freighter *Omsk* on September 8, and a second shipment on the *Poltava* a week later. By mid-October, some forty-two of a planned eighty medium-range missiles

26. "Proceedings of the Hawk's Cay Conference on the Cuban Missile Crisis," Marathon, Florida, March 5–8, 1987, p. 53.

27. See Roger Hilsman, *To Move a Nation: The Politics of Foreign Policy in the Administration of John F. Kennedy* (Garden City, N.Y.: Doubleday, 1967), p. 176. Ball supplied a detailed listing of Soviet military transfers to Cuba.

28. Ibid., p. 180. Note that Bundy referred to "major" offensive capability; he was aware of the IL-28 bombers, which, if that was all that was coming, the administration was prepared to accept as not alone constituting a threat. This matter is discussed under "Stage 4: The Settlement" in this volume.

and associated launch equipment had arrived in Cuba.[29] Construction was under way on four missile complexes, guarded by Soviet mechanized infantry regiments.[30]

The nuclear warheads, it later became clear, almost certainly had not yet arrived, but were to be provided. Curiously, the status of nuclear warheads for the missiles has occasioned more specu-

---

29. I have been using the standard Soviet term "medium-range missiles." In 1962 the United States divided this class of missile into two categories: medium-range (600–1,500 nautical miles; 1,000–2,500 kilometers) and intermediate-range 1,500–3,000 nautical miles; 2,500–5,000 kilometers). The Soviet Union had a medium-range ballistic missile (MRBM) called in the West the SS-4 (Soviet designation R-12), with a maximum range of 1,020 nautical miles, and an intermediate-range ballistic missile (IRBM) called the SS-5 (R-14), with a maximum range of 2,200 nautical miles. The Soviet deployment under way in October 1962 was for twenty-four SS-4 MRBM launchers and sixteen SS-5 IRBM launchers, with two missiles for each launcher (as was standard in the Soviet Union). The IRBMs could reach Washington and New York from Cuba. All forty-two missiles in Cuba in mid-October were SS-4 MRBMs; none of the SS-5 missiles had yet arrived, but the remaining missiles and equipment were en route on five large-hatch ships when the quarantine interdicted their arrival.

In later accounts, particularly by revisionist publicists and scholars, a school of analysis has questioned the honesty of the administration's public statements as to the range of these missiles. Some writers have contended that the real range of the missiles was only a few hundred miles. The chief initial source cited by most of these writers (who include Ronald Steel, David Detzer, Ronald R. Pope, and Barton J. Bernstein) was Robert Hotz, "What Was the Threat?" *Aviation Week and Space Technology,* vol. 77 (November 12, 1962), p. 21. In fact, however, the U.S. intelligence agencies had very good information on the range of these systems, and by noon on October 16 it was clearly established that the MRBMs were SS-4 missiles of 1,020 nautical miles range and not SS-3 missiles of 700 nautical miles range. There was no uncertainty or debate within the administration, and no exaggeration or invention in the information publicly released.

Some scholars of the crisis have also been led by the confusion over "medium-range" missiles into fantasies about a political-military conflict in the Soviet Union. Noting that Khrushchev had, in all his references, spoken only about "medium-range" missiles, these commentators posited the possibility that the appearance in Cuba also of "intermediate-range" missiles may have reflected Soviet military insubordination in going beyond the intentions of the political leadership. Awareness that the Soviet term covers *both* American categories dissolves that speculation.

30. U.S. intelligence on major deliveries of arms to Cuba on the whole was quite good. It was, however, deficient in identifying the buildup of Soviet military personnel, and in particular of the four reinforced mechanized infantry regiments,

lation in recent years than it did during the crisis. The fact is that in October 1962 the United States did not know if there were Soviet nuclear warheads for the missiles in Cuba. It was known that the Soviets were building standard nuclear warhead storage facilities at the missile launch sites, like those in the Soviet Union. The intelligence community had no evidence of the presence in Cuba, or of prior transport to Cuba, of nuclear weapons of any kind. Nonetheless, there was no assurance that warheads had not been brought in without detection, perhaps by submarine or by air. On balance, this was judged improbable, but the policymakers could only be advised that it had to be assumed that the warheads were there, and in due prudence that was the consensus assumption.[31]

---

or "combat teams," each with 1,500–2,500 men and about 100 tanks. The first of these was identified on October 25 by low-level aerial reconnaissance, and the fourth was not identified until November 6, after the peak of the crisis. Full recognition of their size and armament only developed during the first half of November. Yet all had arrived in Cuba between early September and mid-October.

In the first half of October 1962, before the discovery of the missiles, U.S. intelligence estimated 4,500 as the number of Soviet military advisers in Cuba. By the peak of the crisis, the estimate had risen to about 10,000. With the discovery of the four regimental combat teams between October 25 and November 6, the estimate rose again. At first, however, they were estimated to number about 1,000 to 1,500 each; later estimates were 1,500 to 2,500. The actual size of each was probably about 2,500, although most accounts have drawn on the usual estimate at the end of October of about 1,500. By November 19 the intelligence estimate was some 12,000 to 16,000 Soviet military personnel overall, including 8,000 in the four regiments. Later, it was retroactively raised to an estimate that there had been 22,000 Soviet military personnel. Castro years later said the figure was 40,000, and that may be true.

31. A special national intelligence estimate (SNIE) submitted on October 20 stated that "the construction of at least one probable nuclear storage facility [later others were identified] is a strong indication of the Soviet *intent* to provide nuclear warheads. In any case, it is prudent to assume that when the missiles are otherwise operational, nuclear warheads will be available." SNIE 11-19-62, "Major Consequences of Certain U.S. Courses of Action on Cuba," October 20, 1962, p. 2 (Top Secret–Sensitive; now declassified); emphasis added.

Well into the crisis, on October 25, Dean Rusk again raised the question saying "We need to know whether warheads have actually been delivered to Cuba"; but we did not know and the question was not further pursued. See "Summary Record of NSC Executive Committee Meeting No. 5, October 25, 1962, 5 P.M.," p. 1 (Top Secret–Sensitive; now declassified).

Some accounts of the crisis have erroneously referred to the presence of

In fact, there was concrete intelligence that nuclear warheads for the missiles had been loaded on the *Poltava,* one of the large freighters engaged in the missile transfers, which was en route to Cuba at the time the quarantine was imposed. It had been loaded with the missile warheads in Odessa. As with all the missile-transporting ships, the *Poltava* on this occasion declared for a false destination (Algeria), as well as having a false manifest. In this case, however, uniquely, it made a rendezvous in the Atlantic Ocean with three Soviet submarines from the Northern Fleet before heading for Cuba. It was only a few days from Cuba when the quarantine was imposed. The *Poltava* stopped on October 24, and soon returned to the Soviet Union, along with the other four ships carrying missiles and associated equipment, and eleven other ships with other military equipment.

By mid-October the Soviet leaders probably were confident that their gamble on secretly installing the missiles in Cuba was succeeding. Either the Americans were not aware of what was occurring, or, perhaps, the administration was adjusting to the fact and preparing to come to terms with the deployment. They should have been alert to the growing possibility of American detection of the missile deployment activities. On October 15, the very day after the crucial U-2 reconnaissance mission, *Pravda* reported from Havana protests over U.S. overflights of Cuba.

"tactical nuclear weapons" with the Soviet troops in Cuba, and assumed these were intended to counter any invading American forces. There was no intelligence to this effect. These accounts have been based on a misunderstanding, in that the Soviet troops were equipped with FROG short-range rockets, a system that is "nuclear-capable," as are many other rockets and artillery guns. The FROG system was also widely deployed, as in Cuba, for conventional nonnuclear operations.

STAGE 2

The U.S. Decision

ON THE MORNING of October 16 President Kennedy was shown photographs of Soviet SS-4 installations under construction in Cuba, taken two days earlier by a U-2 reconnaissance airplane. He held two long meetings that day, beginning an intensive series of meetings by the group of senior government officials later (from October 23) officially termed the "Ex Comm" (Executive Committee of the National Security Council, or NSC).[32]

A great deal has been written about these seven days of meetings culminating in President Kennedy's public address of October 22. Several of the participants have written accounts or provided information to journalists who soon wrote books on the crisis.[33]

32. The 505th NSC meeting, the only one held during the crisis, was convened on October 22 to ratify the initial decisions. The Executive Committee of the National Security Council was formally established by National Security Action Memorandum 196 on that same day and held its first meeting on October 23. The core of the Ex Comm had, however, been meeting in secrecy since October 16. The final meetings of the ad hoc Ex Comm were held in early 1963 and dealt mostly with policy matters other than the aftermath of the missile crisis. In February 1963 the Ex Comm was dissolved, but it had proved so effective that it was in effect continued with a somewhat narrowed composition as the "Standing Group" of the NSC.

33. There is no need here to list all of these books, as several extensive bibliographies exist; in particular, see Lester H. Brune, *The Missile Crisis of October 1962: A Review of Issues and References* (Claremont, Calif.: Regina Books, 1985). The key volumes by participants were Arthur M. Schlesinger, Jr., *A Thousand Days: John F. Kennedy in the White House* (Boston: Houghton Mifflin, 1965), pp. 794–841; Theodore C. Sorensen, *Kennedy* (New York: Harper and Row, 1965, and Bantam, 1966; quotations in this study from the latter edition, pp. 752–809); and the aforecited books by Robert Kennedy, *Thirteen Days*;

There was never any doubt or debate about the U.S. objective. From the first day, the president never wavered from one basic decision: the Soviet missiles must be removed. There were differing views on the *military* significance of the missiles (Secretary of Defense Robert McNamara downplayed their significance to the strategic balance, while Assistant Secretary of Defense Paul Nitze and the chairman of the Joint Chiefs of Staff, General Maxwell Taylor, stressed their military significance).[34] But more basic was the common judgment that the secret, surreptitious Soviet attempt to install the missiles despite the president's clear warnings could not be accepted. There was little consideration of the fact that the Soviet decision must have been made at least three or four months earlier and could not have been easily reversed in September. But that would not have changed the basic decision.

The key issue for decision, then, over that week was not what the U.S. objective should be, but how to attain it. There were three basic paths: (1) *destroy* the missiles by attacking them; (2) *compel* the Soviet leaders to remove the missiles by pressure; and (3) *induce* the Soviets to remove the missiles by negotiation, probably involving a trade for American concessions. The latter two were not entirely exclusive; there could be pressure *and* negotiation, but there was a clear difference. As General Taylor later characterized the three alternatives, we could "take them out" by our own military action; "squeeze them out" by pressure; or "buy them out" by counterconcessions. The fact that the Soviet action was seen as a political challenge and as the result of duplicity strengthened inclinations not to choose the third alternative.

Schlesinger, *Robert Kennedy*; and Hilsman, *To Move a Nation*. Two other books by seasoned journalists benefited so extensively from background access to official information as to deserve mention here as well; see Elie Abel, *The Missile Crisis* (Philadelphia: J.B. Lippincott, 1966); and Edward Weintal and Charles Bartlett, *Facing the Brink: An Intimate Study of Crisis Diplomacy* (New York: Scribner, 1967). See also Henry M. Pachter, *Collision Course: The Cuban Missile Crisis and Coexistence* (New York: Praeger, 1963); Robert A. Divine, ed., *The Cuban Missile Crisis* (Chicago: Quadrangle Books, 1971); and David Larson, ed., *The Cuban Crisis of 1962: Selected Documents and Chronology* (Boston: Houghton Mifflin, 1963; 2d ed., Lanham, Md.: University Press of America, 1986).

34. See the Appendix, "Commentary on Document D: A Retrospective Evaluation of the Soviet Missiles in Cuba in 1962."

Underlying these deliberations was another significant fact virtually never addressed in American discussions. It had to do with the perceived Soviet motivation. *No one* in the U.S. government believed that the deployment of Soviet missiles was intended to deter a U.S. invasion of Cuba. This was true of all those of us whose task was to estimate Soviet intentions and advise the leadership: the intelligence community, led by the CIA; Ambassador-at-Large Llewellyn E. ("Tommy") Thompson, Jr., personally advising the president and the Ex Comm; and several senior specialists in the Department of State, including myself. Most important, it was also the belief of President Kennedy, Secretary of State Dean Rusk, Secretary of Defense Robert McNamara, National Security Adviser McGeorge Bundy, and other government leaders. Political and expert judgments coincided on this point.

We saw the principal Soviet objective as redressing a strategic inferiority, publicly revealed, and growing in disparity.[35] There was no possibility for an early change in this strategic imbalance through building up intercontinental forces—ICBMs, submarine-launched ballistic missiles (SLBMs), or strategic bombers. While Soviet strategic weapons deployment programs then under way (the SS-7 and SS-8 ICBMs) could help, it would be several years before really satisfactory systems then under development would be ready for deployment (the SS-9 and SS-11 ICBMs, and the SS-N-6, the Soviet equivalent of the Polaris SLBM system). Soviet SS-4 and SS-5 missiles in Cuba could, however, provide an interim substitute, ersatz ICBMs, so to speak.

Beyond that basic agreement as to the strategic rationale under-

35. Deputy Secretary of Defense Roswell L. Gilpatric had disposed of the alleged "missile gap" of American ICBM inferiority in a major speech just a year before (October 21, 1961), in which he stated that the United States could retaliate with equal or greater force even after being subjected to a Soviet first strike. The Gilpatric speech was a carefully considered statement intended to make clear to all, including the Soviet leaders, that the Kennedy administration no longer believed in a missile gap to American disadvantage—that, in fact, there was a growing gap to Soviet disadvantage. On the shift in intelligence estimates and the state of American government assessment, see Raymond L. Garthoff, *Intelligence Assessment and Policymaking: A Decision Point in the Kennedy Administration* (Brookings, 1984).

lying the Soviet decision, there was some divergence of views on whether this was more a defensive political-military measure, or an offensive one. All agreed that the Soviet leaders wanted in general to strengthen their standing in the correlation of forces; most analysts—and political leaders—believed that Khrushchev and the Soviet leadership intended to renew pressures over the Berlin issue from a position of greater strength. Many also believed that the Soviet leaders would use their missiles in Cuba as leverage to place pressure on American military bases around the Soviet Union. As noted earlier, it remains the judgment of most American analysts and historians today that the main Soviet aim in deploying the missiles in Cuba was to bolster Soviet strategic military power and diplomatic-political strength, and that deterrence of an American attack on Cuba was at most a secondary objective.

Notwithstanding the assessment of Soviet strategic inferiority, and the incentive or temptation for Soviet leaders to deploy intermediate-range missiles in Cuba, it was also the unanimous consensus of Soviet affairs experts in the intelligence community and elsewhere in the government that the Soviets would *not* attempt to deploy missiles in Cuba. It was reasoned that while Soviet strategic inferiority might give them an incentive to place missiles in Cuba, it also made that action too risky. In addition, the Soviets had never deployed nuclear weapons outside their own territory (except on naval ships), and exercised very strict controls. Risks even apart from the American reaction were deemed to make such a deployment unlikely. A special national intelligence estimate (SNIE) prepared in mid-September reaffirmed that judgment.[36] There was one notable exception: Director of Central Intelligence McCone, a conservative Republican, believed the Soviets were planning to deploy offensive missiles in Cuba, and so advised the president. During the critical last weeks of September and early October he repeatedly sent such warnings from his honeymoon trip in Europe. But his judgment on this matter was discounted.

Minister of Foreign Affairs Andrei Gromyko visited Washington

36. SNIE 85-3-62, "The Military Buildup in Cuba," September 19, 1962 (Top Secret; now declassified); and see National Intelligence Estimate (NIE) 85-2-62, "The Situation and Prospects in Cuba," August 1, 1962 (Secret; now declassified).

and met with President Kennedy on October 18. This was an important meeting in several respects. Kennedy repeated his warnings of September 4 and 13, but did not ask Gromyko outright whether there were Soviet missiles in Cuba. Gromyko said the Soviet Union would not introduce "offensive arms," but did not say what the Soviet government meant by that term. Kennedy and his advisers considered Gromyko's position to have been duplicitous. They also, after October 16, regarded as disinformation the many assurances that the Soviet Union would not put offensive missiles into Cuba that had earlier been conveyed, including further assurances by Ambassador Dobrynin, most recently on October 13 to former Undersecretary of State Chester Bowles. The most rankling, with the possible exception of Gromyko's evasion, was an assurance through an established and trusted informal channel from Khrushchev personally to the president only a few days earlier. At that time, Robert Kennedy had been told by Soviet Embassy counselor Georgi Bolshakov, after the latter's return from Moscow, that he had been summoned to meet with Khrushchev and Mikoyan and been instructed to convey an assurance to the president that "no missile capable of reaching the United States will be placed in Cuba."[37]

37. See Sorensen, *Kennedy,* p. 753.

Bolshakov had served as an intermediary in a private channel of personal exchanges between Khrushchev and President Kennedy begun a year earlier, so he was regarded as a trusted source. Bolshakov, incidentally, was himself unaware of the missiles when he passed his deceptive message.

For background on Bolshakov's role, see in particular Schlesinger, *Robert Kennedy,* pp. 499–502. (This book is a less well-known source on the missile crisis than the chapter in Schlesinger's *A Thousand Days* but is quite useful on a number of points.)

According to informed American accounts (in particular, Schlesinger, *Robert Kennedy,* p. 527), the Soviets later withdrew Bolshakov after his role had been revealed by disclosure of his pre-crisis unwitting deception on the missiles in a news column by Joseph Alsop. Robert Kennedy even wrote him a personal letter of appreciation. Ibid.

Bolshakov's role remained, of course, a carefully kept secret in Moscow. At least some quarters in the Soviet establishment believe that his departure from Washington was engineered by the United States. I have been told by a Kremlin "insider" of that time that among themselves Khrushchev had told the following anecdote: first, he had been asked by the Americans to withdraw the missiles,

The second aspect of Gromyko's visit was a proposal to the president for a summit meeting of the two leaders, some time following the American congressional elections in November. Although Kennedy made a vaguely positive response, he instructed Ambassador Thompson to tell Ambassador Dobrynin that same night at dinner that a summit would not be appropriate under current conditions and would require proper preparations. U.S. advisers and political leaders saw the Soviet proposal for a summit, and the earlier assurances that the Soviet Union would not cause any problems for the Kennedy administration before the November 7 elections, as signs that by the time of a summit meeting in late November or December, Khrushchev planned to make publicly known that the Soviet missiles were already deployed and operational in Cuba, and buttressed by this new position of strength, to make new demands, probably on the status of Berlin.[38]

Later critics of the president's handling of the crisis have asked why he did not tell Gromyko about the missiles, or send a private message to Khrushchev, and give the Soviet leader an opportunity to save face by withdrawing the missiles quietly. Ambassador Charles E. ("Chip") Bohlen had suggested a letter to Khrushchev on October 18. Kennedy and several of his close advisers did try for two days, October 18 to 20, to draft such a letter.[39] But they were unable to find a formula that would be sufficiently persuasive without itself precipitating a crisis. Moreover, there was a general consensus that it would be undesirable to let the Soviets take the

---

and did. Then he was asked to withdraw the IL-28 bombers, and did. Finally, he was asked to withdraw Bolshakov, and did—but put his foot down at that point, saying, "All right, Bolshakov too, but nothing more!"

38. A plenary meeting of the Central Committee of the Communist Party of the Soviet Union was already scheduled to meet in Moscow on November 19–23. Some have speculated that Khrushchev wanted to have an international triumph from his missile venture by then. Others have noted that the SS-5 IRBMs would not have been fully operational by that date, and therefore the missiles could not yet be revealed. It is not known if Khrushchev was seeking to bring matters to a head as early as that Central Committee plenum. The general judgment that he planned at some point suddenly to make known the deployment of the missiles and to make political capital of the surprise move was almost certainly valid.

39. See Schlesinger, *Robert Kennedy,* p. 513.

initiative. I believe the decision not to do so was sound. In any case, the decision not to raise the matter privately with Khrushchev (and still less with Gromyko) was deliberate and considered.

Within a few days the members of the Ex Comm and the president himself decided on what they regarded as the middle course: a blockade (termed a "quarantine" to avoid the status of belligerency entailed under international law by imposing a naval blockade) to interdict any further shipment of Soviet offensive arms to Cuba. Advocates of an American air attack on the missile facilities (and Cuban air force bases and other large airfields, also considered militarily necessary) were not helped in their case by the U.S. Air Force judgment that this would require 500 sorties—and that even then there could be no guarantee that all the missiles would be destroyed, or civilians spared. Contrary to Soviet and Cuban claims, there was no U.S. plan under way for an invasion of Cuba. Contingency plans existed, but *not* a plan that had been adopted. There was, however, some military and political sentiment during the crisis deliberations that following an air strike it would probably be necessary to mount an invasion of the island to destroy Cuban military power, and that it would be desirable at the same time to end Castro's rule. An air strike remained a possible recourse if the quarantine was not successful in inducing the Soviet leaders to agree to remove the missiles, but it seemed better to begin with more limited actions and then, if necessary, escalate. Also, the third alternative, a diplomatic negotiating path, was in fact expected to develop. There was, however, reluctance to think in terms of American concessions in general, as well as any specific terms. The only top adviser who did so with any passion, Adlai Stevenson, was as a result considered too much a "dove." The leading "hawk," calling for an immediate air strike and defeat of Castro's rule, was former Secretary of State Dean Acheson, called upon for advice in the first days of the crisis. But others also held this view, especially in the first few days, when it was the majority view. Fortunately, there was a full week for deliberation.[40]

It should be stressed, as many have observed, that the ability to

40. The current political connotations of the terms "hawks" and "doves" originated during the missile crisis.

devote an entire week to deliberation and decision free of public
pressure, and free of Soviet action or interaction, was crucial. It
was also unique; no other past crisis has had, and none in the future
can be expected to have, such a lengthy period for decision free
from external and domestic political pressures.

The overriding issue in the first phase was to decide on the
precise objective and course of action to deal with the surreptitious
Soviet deployment of medium- and intermediate-range missiles in
Cuba. This stage was marked by secret meetings, most held in
Undersecretary of State Ball's office in the State Department to
avoid the attention that arrivals for meetings at the White House
would entail.[41] "Scenarios" providing action-response sequences
were developed for three major alternative courses of action: a
"political path," for a diplomatic deal with the Soviet Union,
probably through a summit meeting with Khrushchev; a "quarantine," a selective and possibly gradually tightening blockade to
prevent the arrival of more missiles and to compel Soviet withdrawal of those already in Cuba; and an "air-strike option," to
destroy the missiles and launch facilities, probably with land
invasion to follow to ensure no reconstitution of a military threat
to the United States—also, of course, disposing of Castro once and
for all. Some members of the Ex Comm sought limited advice from
their own staffs as the week progressed, and assistance was
discreetly provided for some scenario-writing. But by and large
the order of the day was to limit participation to the select senior
officials in frequent and often lengthy meetings. By the end of the
week a great deal of staff support for certain key diplomatic actions
was required: preparations for rallying the support of the Organization of American States (OAS) for the quarantine; preparations
for last-hour consultations with key allies; preparations to call a
UN Security Council meeting; preparations for key congressional
consultations; and the like.[42] Military contingency planning was

41. Ball's office was referred to by some participants as the "think tank,"
coining a term later applied widely to intellectual centers cogitating and advising
on policy matters.

42. For example, in the forty-eight hours from midnight October 20 to midnight
October 22, the State Department, working around the clock, transmitted fifteen

under way, and preparations were made for implementing a blockade.

During the first stage, one key element was predicting the Soviet response or, more accurately, estimating the range of possible Soviet responses, and the American actions that could help to channel such responses in desired directions and away from the most dangerous and undesired ones. The analyses and estimates of Soviet responses were all keyed to the alternative U.S. actions and related scenarios.[43]

Once the president had spoken, American attention shifted from our decision to the Soviet response. And the Soviet leadership suddenly realized it was in a first-class crisis.

---

separate presidential letters or messages to 441 recipients, with appropriate instructions on delivery, gave oral briefings to ninety-five foreign ambassadors, and drafted or participated in drafting and dispatched most messages and the texts of the U.S. proposals for the OAS and UN forums and appropriate background messages to various embassies—including a warning to 134 U.S. embassies and consulates to take precautions against possible hostile demonstrations following the president's address.

43. Ambassadors Llewellyn E. Thompson, Jr., and (until his departure for Paris on October 19) Charles E. Bohlen gave their expert advice. Two special national intelligence estimates—SNIE 11-18-62, "Soviet Reactions to Certain US Courses of Action on Cuba," October 19, and SNIE 11-19-62 "Major Consequences of Certain U.S. Courses of Action on Cuba," October 20 (both originally Top Secret–Sensitive; now declassified)—represented the best judgment of the intelligence community on Soviet responses.

Interestingly, the intelligence estimates considered an air strike and gradually escalating military actions *more* likely to prompt local Soviet involvement in military counteractions than a prompt all-out invasion. See SNIE 11-19-62, p. 9.

The Confrontation

PRESIDENT KENNEDY's address on October 22 had firmly set the objective of the dismantling and withdrawal of Soviet offensive weapons from Cuba. He intentionally directed attention at Moscow, and ignored Castro and the Cuban role.[44]

The United States had prepared carefully for rapid action by the Organization of American States, including direct communication to the Mexican president and foreign minister while they were traveling in the Far East. The seriousness of the Soviet and communist challenge (as it was seen and depicted), and the strength of the U.S. government's resolve, contributed to a unanimous OAS vote on October 23 condemning the missiles as a threat to the peace and calling for their removal. This was an even better outcome than had been anticipated in Washington. There had been confidence in the State Department in obtaining the support of a majority, even the two-thirds majority needed for an OAS imprimatur on the quarantine, but not in rallying a unanimous vote. In the United Nations Security Council there was more hesitancy, but the Soviet failure until October 28 to acknowledge publicly the presence of its missiles in Cuba, counterposed to convincing American photographic evidence, weakened the presentation of the Soviet case claiming that it was a normal and justified action to

---

44. Consideration had been given to approaching Castro and seeking by threats—and possibly incentives if he broke with Moscow—to work on getting the missiles out through a Cuban reversal. In retrospect as well as in judgment at the time, as an alternative to facing the Soviet leaders head-on that course would probably have been ineffective and unwise.

station forces in the territory of a friendly state. Other key neutral states, as well as allies, also gave support.[45]

The U.S. leaders were initially concerned above all about two things: Would the Soviet leaders attempt to send military shipments through the quarantine blockade and challenge the U.S. Navy? And would the Soviet leaders attempt to build counterpressure elsewhere, for example by imposing a "quarantine" blockade of West Berlin, or a threat against the American intermediate-range missiles in Turkey?

The first of the appended memoranda is a hasty analysis I prepared on October 23 in response to a request by Walt W. Rostow, then head of the policy-planning council in the State Department. While it represented my personal view, it provides something of a feel for the thinking at the time on both Soviet motivation in placing the missiles in Cuba and on the range of counteractions the Soviet leaders might consider. I sought to indicate the "cards" they might see themselves holding.[46] (I did not, incidentally, believe they would respond by counterescalation in Berlin or Turkey, and so argued, although not in this memorandum.)

From all indications the Soviet leaders were caught by surprise by President Kennedy's speech on October 22. Ambassador Dobrynin, called in by Secretary Rusk and given a copy of the speech just an hour before it was delivered, arrived in a relaxed mood but left "ashen-faced" and "visibly shaken." Robert Kennedy went to see him the next evening and Dobrynin still "seemed very shaken, out of the picture," without instructions, and uninformed as to any instructions that might have been given to Soviet ships about stopping short of the quarantine line (the main point on which Kennedy was hoping to get some indication).[47]

---

45. In a notable example, on October 23 the American ambassadors in leftist Guinea, and in Senegal, were instructed to request that no permission be given to the Soviet Union for air-landing rights at Conakry and Dakar. Both countries agreed to the American request, foreclosing to the Soviet Union the option of air supply of key military equipment to Cuba.

46. See Appendix document A.

47. For Kennedy's visit, see Schlesinger, *A Thousand Days,* p. 817. Dobrynin's

By coincidence Foreign Minister Gromyko was just departing from the United States to return to Moscow on the afternoon of October 22; his departure remarks were routine, and obviously he had not been either summoned home earlier or told to remain.[48]

It remains unknown what the Soviets had observed during the American activities of October 16 through 22, and what meaning they ascribed to whatever activities they had become aware of. One would assume that they had noticed the greatly intensified aerial surveillance of Cuba, although that information might not have gone beyond their intelligence watch institutions. They should have been able to pick up some of the preliminary U.S. military movements at sea, by the U.S. Air Force, and in Florida despite our efforts to preserve an atmosphere of normalcy—although, again, taken alone these might not have attracted political attention in Moscow. Some of the military moves were explicable in terms of a previously announced amphibious exercise in the Caribbean. Finally, inasmuch as several alert American newsmen and one ally (Great Britain) became aware of the unique pattern of secret high-level government meetings, one might assume that Soviet intelligence in Washington would have gotten wind of something unusual too. But we don't know, and there is no indication from Soviet behavior that they had realized or even suspected what was under way.

The president's speech was of course the primary focus for Soviet attention. In it, he disclosed that U.S. intelligence had discovered the missiles in Cuba six days earlier. The president referred to the MRBMs, the IRBMs, and "jet bombers, capable of carrying nuclear weapons." He recalled his own September warnings, and cited public and private deceptive Soviet assurances that seemed to deny that offensive missiles would be sent to Cuba, and the surreptitious nature of the deployment. He characterized "their

reaction to Rusk's message was noted by several news correspondents who observed him enter and leave; see also Kennedy, *Thirteen Days,* pp. 52–53.

48. When word reached Washington that Gromyko would meet the press before boarding his flight, there was excited speculation by some that he might make some dramatic preemptive statement about the missiles in Cuba, presumably having learned the subject of the president's address. There was thus considerable relief when he made merely routine remarks on departure.

sudden, clandestine decision to station strategic weapons for the
first time outside of Soviet soil" as "a deliberately provocative and
unjustified change in the status quo which cannot be accepted by
this country." He called upon Khrushchev "to halt and eliminate
this clandestine, reckless, and provocative threat to world peace
. . . and to join in an historic effort to end the perilous arms race
and transform the history of man."[49]

The quarantine to interdict any further transfer of offensive
weapons to Cuba was announced, although without specifying
when it would take effect. It was identified as one of a series of
"*initial* steps," along with an immediate call for convening of the
OAS, and an emergency meeting of the UN Security Council to
seek "the prompt dismantling and withdrawal of all offensive
weapons in Cuba, under the supervision of United Nations observ-
ers" as a precondition for lifting the quarantine.[50]

The overt nuclear element of the confrontation was contained
in Kennedy's declaration that "it shall be the policy of this nation
to regard any nuclear missile launched from Cuba against any
nation in the Western Hemisphere as an attack by the Soviet Union
on the United States, requiring a full retaliatory response upon the
Soviet Union."[51]

Finally, although virtually never noted in American commentaries on the crisis, the Soviet (and Cuban) leaders would have
taken particular note of another passage of several paragraphs
addressed to "the captive people of Cuba," declaring that "your
leaders are no longer Cuban leaders inspired by Cuban ideals. They
are puppets and agents of an international conspiracy which has
turned Cuba against your friends and neighbors in the Americas—
and turned it into the first Latin American country to become a
target for nuclear war—the first Latin American country to have
these weapons on its soil. . . . Your lives and land are being used
as pawns by those who deny you freedom. . . . I have no doubt
that most Cubans today look forward to the time when they will be

49. "Radio and Television Report to the American People on the Soviet Arms
Buildup in Cuba, October 22, 1962," *Public Papers: Kennedy, 1962*, pp. 806–08.

50. Ibid., pp. 807–08; emphasis added.

51. Ibid., p. 808.

truly free. . . . And then shall Cuba be welcomed back to the society of free nations. . . ."[52]

The Soviet leaders certainly understood that President Kennedy was now publicly committed to the removal of their missiles from Cuba and was instituting "initial steps" to cut off any further buildup. They probably knew or were quickly briefed on the fact that an effective quarantine meant that none of the IRBM missiles, and more important none of the nuclear warheads for any of the missiles, had yet reached Cuba. The fact that the nuclear warheads were at that very time en route at sea still several days from Cuba may have led the Soviet leaders to believe that the United States had timed the action to prevent the arrival of the warheads—rather than realizing that the Ex Comm believed it must assume the nuclear warheads were already in Cuba. But this consideration affected at most their judgment as to whether a viable "freeze" short of the planned deployment, but not involving withdrawal, might be negotiable. The dramatic American threat of full retaliation for any missile fired from Cuba, which attracted so much attention in the West, and which was undoubtedly desirable as a sign of American determination, was irrelevant to Moscow's calculations. I am sure that under *no* contingency did the Soviet leadership contemplate actually firing its Cuban missiles, even if the warheads had been there.

Of much greater concern in Moscow was whether the United States would now use the Soviet missiles as an excuse to invade Cuba. It was from this standpoint that they probably weighed the president's words about a "captive" Cuba and the American call for its freedom. They had no way of knowing that Kennedy had rejected even stiffer language hinting at the removal of Castro— what they did hear seemed ominous enough.[53]

In addition, the Soviet leaders no doubt reevaluated such facts as the planned American amphibious exercise aimed at liberating the Caribbean island of Vieques near Puerto Rico from a fictional dictator "Ortsac" (Castro spelled backwards).

52. Ibid., p. 809.
53. See Sorensen, *Kennedy*, p. 789.

The American success the next day in gaining unanimous support of its OAS allies was undoubtedly a shock for the Soviets. What they had hoped would be an anti-Yanqui backlash in Latin America at the American action against Cuba evaporated.

Another event almost certainly noted in Moscow, but *not* in Washington, was the coincidence that on that very day, October 22, with ceremonial fanfare, the Jupiter missiles in Turkey were turned over to Turkish command.[54] This fact, remarkably, has only recently been recognized; it was not by the American leaders at the time. It explains why Khrushchev had felt it a timely thing to complain about to Ambassador Kohler on October 16.

The very hour of the president's speech was chosen for instituting a Defense Condition (Defcon) 3 alert of all major U.S. commands and for shifting from limited military preparations under wraps to open all-out buildup of the contingent air-strike and invasion forces of the U.S. Army, Navy, Air Force, and Marines. This alert action was both incidental to the shift to open operations and intended to demonstrate the seriousness of U.S. preparations for possible further military steps beyond the quarantine. An alert of all major commands had not been activated since the Korean War and must have been regarded seriously in Moscow.

Among other highly visible actions in implementing this alert on October 22 was the dispersal of the B-47 medium bomber force to some thirty-three civilian airports. An extraordinary further signal reached the Soviet leadership just forty-eight hours later. Unprecedented actions were taken by the U.S. Strategic Air Command (SAC). SAC was generated to still higher alert, Defcon 2, for the first time ever, on October 24. This involved a further and unprecedented intensification of combat readiness measures, including a significant increase in the armed airborne alert portion of the B-52 heavy bomber force and shift to military alert status of ICBM launchers undergoing checkout or other off-line status.[55] Most of this would, of course, have been observed in due course by one or

---

54. Murray Marder dug this fact out through diligent research into declassified records.

55. One out of every eight B-52s was always in the air, armed with nuclear

another means of Soviet information collection. But in this case there was a unique difference: the SAC full-alert process was conducted "in the clear" rather than in normal encoded messages. Soviet communications interception personnel must have been shocked suddenly to hear all the alert orders from Omaha and a steady stream of responses from bomber units reporting their attainment of alert posture, including nuclear-armed flights poised for attack on the Soviet Union. And the Soviet political and military leaders must have been puzzled and alarmed at this flaunting of the American strategic superiority, so great that the United States could afford to ignore normal operational security in order to drive home the extent of its power.

Equally extraordinary, and not known in Moscow, was that this remarkable display of American power was unauthorized by and unknown to the president, the secretary of defense, the chairman of the JCS, and the Ex Comm as they so carefully calibrated and controlled action in the intensifying confrontation. The decision for this bold action was taken by General Thomas Powers, commander-in-chief of SAC, on his own initiative. He had been ordered to go on full alert, and he did so. No one had told him *how* to do it, and he decided to "rub it in." Nor did he even inform higher authority after the fact (or, if he did inform General Curtis LeMay, chief of staff of the U.S. Air Force, LeMay in turn did not tell anyone in the government leadership). When I mentioned this incident to a recent conference of former Ex Comm members (including then National Security Adviser McGeorge Bundy and then Secretary of Defense Robert McNamara) I discovered none had been aware until now of this happening.[56]

Caught unaware, the Soviet leaders' first inclination was to reassess the situation, probe at possible ways to recoup as much

---

weapons and ready to strike upon order; aerial tankers were ready to service the entire bomber fleet. Polaris submarines in port went to sea.

56. I was first told about this action soon after the crisis by Major General (then Colonel) George J. Keegan, Jr., then SAC chief of intelligence, who was present when General Powers gave the order and it was executed.

My reference to the alert at the conference was later reported by J. Anthony Lukas, "Class Reunion: Kennedy's Men Relive the Cuban Missile Crisis," *New York Times Magazine*, August 30, 1987, p. 51.

as they could, and in the meantime play for time, and avoid any provocative action that might trigger further American actions. Not until fourteen hours after the president's speech did the Soviet government issue a public statement sharply critical of the American actions, but silent on Soviet moves.

One action, however, was undertaken without delay. Colonel Oleg Penkovsky of Soviet Military Intelligence, an American (and British) spy in Moscow, was immediately arrested on October 22. Penkovsky had been under suspicion by Soviet counterintelligence for some time but they had permitted him to continue at liberty (under close surveillance) in order to see if there were other Soviet agents in a network and to monitor contacts with his Central Intelligence Agency (CIA) and Secret Intelligence Service (SIS) handlers in the U.S. and U.K. embassies in Moscow. Soviet counterintelligence did not know, however, until his arrest and interrogation precisely what he had turned over to the Western intelligence services. In particular, they did not know if he had acquired and passed on information on the Cuban missile deployment. In fact, while from April 1961 to September 1962 Penkovsky had provided a tremendous amount of important military information, he had not been aware of and been able to pass on anything about the missiles in Cuba. But this was not yet known to the Soviet military, intelligence, and political leaders on October 22.[57]

57. Some intelligence provided by Penkovsky was useful background information during the crisis. In particular, he had provided information on the Soviet missile forces, including the SS-4 and SS-5 systems. U.S. intelligence identification of the sites in Cuba, however, was based on familiarity with such sites in the USSR from overhead reconnaissance. A British writer, in a popular history of the British Secret Intelligence Service (SIS), has written an account of the Cuban missile crisis strewn with errors and grossly exaggerating Penkovsky's role. See Anthony Verrier, *Through the Looking Glass: British Foreign Policy in an Age of Illusions* (New York: W. W. Norton, 1983), pp. 193, 221–43.

Two American intelligence-associated commentators have also credited Penkovsky with providing information that was valuable to the United States in the missile crisis. That is correct, although the implied degree of value is exaggerated. See Frank Gibney, Introduction, in Oleg Penkovskiy, *The Penkovskiy Papers* (Garden City, N.Y.: Doubleday, 1965), pp. 4, 17. And without explicitly naming Penkovsky, CIA Director Richard Helms had him particularly in mind in a public reference; see Chalmers M. Roberts, " 'Well-Placed Russians' Aided U.S. in Cuban Missile Crisis," *Washington Post,* April 16, 1971. Despite the title of the

Penkovsky's arrest, promptly known to the U.S. and British intelligence services and thus to CIA Director John McCone, was regarded strictly as an operational intelligence matter and was not even brought to the attention of the Ex Comm.

If the significance of one important operational detail had been evaluated differently by Penkovsky's CIA and SIS handlers, however, it could have had a profound effect in greatly heightening tension in the crisis. I am disclosing this matter here for the first time, and with a caveat on its provenance. I had been involved in intelligence analysis and specifically in the evaluation of Penkovsky's materials from the outset of his reporting in the spring of 1961. One of the key CIA clandestine service officers responsible for directly managing the Penkovsky case, whom I had come to know well as a reliable person, is my source for this information. He told me in strict confidence soon after the event. In the nature of such things, and given both continuing secrecy pledges and diminishing sources after a quarter of a century, I have not been able to confirm this report, but also not to disconfirm it. I believe it to be true.

Penkovsky maintained communication with his American and British contacts in Moscow principally through "dead drops," places where material was left to be picked up by the other party. Nonverbal telephone signals were used to indicate that such drops had been made. In addition, Penkovsky was given a few standard coded telephonic signals for use in emergencies, including one to be used if he was about to be arrested, and also one to be used in the ultimate contingency: imminent war. When he was being arrested, at his apartment, he had time to send a telephonic signal— but chose to use the signal for an imminent Soviet attack! This seemingly bizarre act rings true. Penkovsky had always been a man with unusual self-importance (for example, he had asked his SIS handlers, while in London on an official trip in 1961, to be introduced to Queen Elizabeth, and to be whisked to Washington

article, what Helms is quoted as saying, correctly, is that the United States was aided by material in "intelligence files" provided earlier by "U-2 photography of the Soviet Union" and "a number of well-placed and courageous Russians who helped us," including "a wealth of information on Soviet missile systems."

to meet President Kennedy; and he liked to wear British and American colonels' uniforms at his clandestine debriefing sessions when he was traveling in the West). He had tried to egg the Western powers on to more aggressive actions against the Soviet Union during the Berlin crisis in 1961. So when he was about to go down, he evidently decided to play Samson and bring the temple down on everyone else as well. Normally, such an attempt would have been feckless. But October 22, 1962, was not a normal day. Fortunately, his Western intelligence handlers, at the operational level, after weighing a dilemma of great responsibility, decided not to credit Penkovsky's final signal and suppressed it. Not even the higher reaches of the CIA were informed of Penkovsky's provocative farewell. And so the tale has, until now, remained untold.

The Soviet leaders sought to maintain a low-key atmosphere in Moscow. While probably stemming chiefly from a desire by Khrushchev and the inner core of leaders to keep decisions in their own hands, not even the whole of the Presidium (the 1962 Politburo) was assembled—those members resident elsewhere in the Soviet Union because they held regional leadership positions were not summoned to Moscow during the whole ensuing week of crisis. (Mikoyan, on vacation, was promptly called back and arrived in Moscow on the 23rd.) On October 23 five top leaders—Khrushchev, Leonid Brezhnev, Frol Kozlov, Aleksei Kosygin, and Mikoyan—attended an opera performance, demonstrating their own solidarity and seeking to show normalcy. After the performance, Khrushchev made the gesture of visiting backstage the American basso Jerome Hines, displaying an absence of animus toward the American people. Life in Moscow, including government working patterns and rehearsals for the annual November 7 anniversary parade, was normal. Diplomatic travelers were called back to Moscow as a precautionary measure, and most trip requests denied, but diplomatic life was also normal. Similarly, while Soviet and Warsaw Pact alerts were prominently announced on October 23, they were in fact minimal in impact, mainly involving largely symbolic measures such as cancelling leaves. There were no major redeployments or high-readiness measures of the strategic missile force, air force, army, or navy.

Within a few days, it had become clear that the Soviet leaders would not either challenge the quarantine at sea or mount a countermove. The ships carrying additional missiles and military equipment stopped and then turned back. There was no escalatory initiative elsewhere.

On the other hand, construction of the missile bases in Cuba continued, and there was no Soviet diplomatic or other move indicating any readiness to withdraw them. Indeed the Soviets still continued publicly to deny their very existence. The debate in the Ex Comm therefore turned to renewed consideration of additional steps to induce or compel removal of the missiles. The quarantine middle course had served a useful role, but advocates of a need for more diplomatic flexibility on the one hand, and for an air strike against the missiles on the other, the doves and hawks, again began to urge new decisions.

The most hotly debated issue proposed by some as a diplomatic alternative to an air strike was negotiation of a trade of mutual concessions, in particular the idea that as a counterpart to Soviet withdrawal of its missiles from Cuba, the United States might agree to remove its comparable intermediate-range missiles from Turkey—adjoining the Soviet Union, just as Cuba virtually adjoined the United States, with only ninety miles of water between.[58] This idea had arisen very early in the secret deliberation of the first week, and publicly in the second week, of the crisis. On October 25 it was advocated by the distinguished commentator Walter Lippman. His proposal of the idea led many, perhaps also in Moscow, to wonder if it was a trial balloon by the administration. It was not.

The major objection was that the missiles in Turkey were there pursuant to a NATO decision and bilateral U.S.-Turkish agreements, and the United States would appear to be giving up a commitment to NATO in order to relieve itself of a threat, and moreover one that NATO countries in Europe had all faced for

58. Another proposed concession, suggested by Stevenson but quickly dismissed by the president, was a U.S. return of Guantánamo Bay and its base to Cuba in exchange for Soviet withdrawal of its missiles and all other military presence.

several years.[59] More basically, there was strong sentiment against making a concession because it would show a lack of resolve to compel the Soviets to retract their unwarranted and surreptitious deployment. On the other side, it was argued that the missiles in Turkey were obsolete, should be removed in any case (and were planned to be removed as soon as it could be arranged diplomatically), and that it was absurd to intensify a confrontation that risked war for the sake of some unneeded and unwanted hardware.

The second of the appended memoranda was written on October 25, again to Walt Rostow.[60] I believed that the Soviet leaders would back down and withdraw the missiles in the face of continued firmness and pressure. I was "hawkish" on the question of compelling this outcome, rather than seeking to induce it through concessions. On the other hand, while prepared to contemplate use of military force if necessary, I was not among the hawks who *sought* to use military force or wished to set the extirpation of

59. NATO had decided late in 1957, when Soviet primacy in missilery first seemed to portend a missile gap, to station American-made intermediate-range missiles in Europe. Great Britain and the United States had concluded an arrangement that had provided sixty Thor IRBM missiles to Britain. Italy agreed in 1959 to take thirty Jupiter IRBM missiles, and Turkey fifteen. The whole process of negotiation, training, constructing facilities, and the like took several years. Meanwhile the missiles became increasingly obsolete, and other, more suitable weapons, ICBMs and SLBMs, became available in rapidly growing numbers. In August 1962 the British had announced that the Thors were being phased out, and they were all out by December. In Italy the Jupiters had become operational in 1961–62. As earlier noted, in Turkey, by remarkable coincidence, the actual turnover of the first Jupiter missiles to the Turkish armed forces (the warheads, of course, remained under U.S. control in all cases) occurred on October 22, 1962—the very day of Kennedy's quarantine announcement. This fact was not, however, known to him and to the other top American leaders, who had instead been thinking of phasing out these missiles as obsolete. President Kennedy had urged that this be done on several earlier occasions in 1961 and 1962, most recently in August. Accounts suggesting that the president was shocked to find that the Jupiters were still in Turkey, or that earlier orders by him for their removal had not been carried out, are in error.

60. See Appendix document B.
This memorandum was circulated to some Ex Comm members, and I was told that Robert Kennedy had read it and spoken approvingly of it. It was, incidentally, a unique and heady experience for staff officers to write memoranda, uncleared by anyone, that were circulated only hours later to top decisionmakers.

communism in Cuba as a new, more far-reaching objective.[61] But in opposing a "trade" of missile bases, I was a hawk. The third memorandum, written on October 27 for Alexis Johnson, also makes that clear. It was written principally to support the "hang tough" school in the State Department, to which he too belonged, and which was prepared to resort to an air strike if necessary to effect the elimination of the missiles in Cuba, while opposing a negotiated trade of missile bases.[62]

One important aspect of the internal debate in mid-week, around October 24–25, was the possibility of tightening the quarantine to cover not only all military supplies but above all petroleum, as a way to squeeze Cuba and prevent a stalemate. Even before the president's address of October 22, when the quarantine option was being thought through, consideration was given to the possibility of a Soviet counterblockade of Berlin and to whether Berlin or Cuba would be more vulnerable to a cutoff of outside food and energy supplies. By the end of the week, however, concern had focused on how to bring the crisis to a head before the Soviet missiles already in Cuba became accepted as an element in the status quo.[63] Accordingly, the emphasis had shifted to either a diplomatic deal involving a tradeoff of missile bases, or unilateral American military action to destroy the missile complexes.

No one in the Ex Comm, in the period before October 26, even posed the possibility of a diplomatic resolution based on an American commitment not to invade Cuba—not because of opposition to the idea, but because none of the president's counselors conceived of that as a trade the Soviet Union would seek or settle for. Nonetheless the president himself was thinking along those lines by midweek. On October 25 President Kennedy, in a conversation

61. For example, I vividly recall one small "caucus" meeting of a few hard-line State Department officers (and Dorothy Fosdick, then chief aide to Senator Henry Jackson) with Dean Acheson, in which I was the only non-hawk uncomfortably present.

62. See Appendix document C.

63. On October 26 I was tasked after the Ex Comm meeting to draw up a memorandum on the military significance of the missiles in Cuba. See Appendix document D. A commentary on the memorandum and retrospective evaluation of the missiles follows the document.

with British Prime Minister Harold Macmillan, wondered whether some acceptable political proposal could be made, such as a trade for withdrawal of the Soviet missiles of some international guarantee for Cuba against invasion.[64]

And on October 26, at the sixth meeting of the Ex Comm, the president noted the Brazilian proposal at the UN General Assembly for a guarantee of the territorial integrity of all Latin American states (and for their denuclearization), and asked if the United States should commit itself not to invade Cuba. Secretary Rusk replied that the United States had already committed itself not to invade Cuba under the UN Charter and the Rio Treaty of 1947.[65]

Preparations for an invasion, as well as an air strike, continued to be made as a possible recourse, if necessary, to resolve the problem. In addition to military preparations (including mobilization of military civil government teams for occupation tasks), on October 25 President Kennedy authorized a program, christened "Bugle Call," to prepare leaflets to drop over Cuba, in anticipation of an invasion. By the 27th some five million leaflets had been printed in Spanish and the U.S. Air Force was ready to drop them whenever ordered. The order was, of course, never given and the leaflets were presumably later destroyed.

One important area on which the American policymakers and their advisers had virtually no information during the crisis, and scarcely more even after twenty-five years, was the state of planning within the Soviet leadership. Contemporary sources included official Soviet statements, the Soviet press, reports from the American Embassy in Moscow, and appearances of Soviet leaders. On October 23, as earlier noted, five of the top leaders attended the opera; on the 26th five attended a concert; on October 28, as the critical phase ended, ten top leaders demonstratively again together attended the theater (Khrushchev, Kozlov, Brezhnev, Mikhail A. Suslov, Kosygin, Mikoyan, Dmitri S. Polyansky,

64. Memorandum of conversation between President John F. Kennedy and Prime Minister Harold Macmillan, October 25, 1962; and see Harold Macmillan, *At the End of the Day: 1961–1963* (Harper and Row, 1973), pp. 210–11.

65. "Summary Record of NSC Executive Committee Meeting No. 6, October 26, 1962, 10:00 A.M.," p. 2 (Top Secret–Sensitive; now declassified).

Petr N. Demichev, Leonid F. Ilychev, and Aleksandr N. Shelepin).
But did that signal real unity, or a facade arranged precisely to
cover up real differences?[66]

"Kremlinologists" in Washington picked up, three weeks later
when it was first published, the intriguing fact that on October 25
the Ukrainian Supreme Soviet had renamed the town of Khrushchev, Kremges—an apparent slap at the first secretary. The newspaper *Izvestiya,* edited by Khrushchev's son-in-law Aleksei Adzhubei, was notably more ready than *Pravda* to seek a compromise
solution to the crisis; the military newspaper *Red Star,* on the other
hand, was notably more militant and intransigent. For example,
on October 27, when Khrushchev was trying to make a deal
involving *no* reference to any American missile bases, and the
Presidium consensus sought a trade for U.S. missiles in Turkey,
Red Star published an article referring to the U.S. demands for
removal of Soviet weaponry (not yet identified specifically as
missiles) from Cuba and truculently asked, "Why then not remove
American weaponry and troops from the *hundreds* of military bases
surrounding the Soviet Union?"[67]

On November 3 the old defeated Stalinist Marshal Klimenty
Ye. Voroshilov was resurrected from political oblivion to be
identified as author of an article in *Pravda* extolling Khrushchev's
handling of the crisis.[68]

At the same time, there were many signs that the price for
support of conservative party leaders on the Cuban affair was an
abatement of Khrushchev's internal political destalinization campaign. On November 1 *Pravda* had reprinted an editorial article
from the Mongolian Communist party newspaper *Unen* criticizing

66. Later, in his unofficial memoirs, Khrushchev remarked that on one of
these occasions—probably October 26—he suggested to his colleagues that they
attend the Bolshoi Theater to have a calming effect on the public. And he added,
"We were trying to disguise our own anxiety, which was intense." He does not
mention divisions in the leadership. See Talbott, ed. and trans., *Khrushchev
Remembers* (1970), p. 497.

67. A. Leont'yev, "Ashes and a Cold Shower," *Krasnaya Zvezda* (Red Star),
October 27, 1962; emphasis added.

68. K. Voroshilov, "The Cause of Great October Lives and Triumphs,"
Pravda, November 3, 1962.

the lately deposed Mongolian party secretary D. Tumur-Ochir for attempting to "use the struggle against the remnants of the cult of personality for his own far-reaching purposes"—precisely the concern of some Moscow party leaders over Khrushchev's designs and machinations.[69] Khrushchev also had to shift his position on October 25 from neutrality to support for China in the Indian-Chinese border war that had broken out during the missile crisis.

Several Western Kremlinological studies of Soviet politics have examined the Soviet press and internal policy turns of 1962 and 1963 in detail, and focused on such indications as these.[70] Most of this analysis was, however, either not available during the missile crisis or not brought to the attention of the harassed Executive Committee.

Particular attention was given to signs of any divergence between the body of political leaders (and Khrushchev in particular) and the military leadership. Marshal Rodion Ya. Malinovsky, the defense minister, was not a member of the Presidium.

On November 7, at the parade on the anniversary of the revolution, Marshal Malinovsky praised Khrushchev personally for his role in saving the peace in the Caribbean crisis, and endorsed peaceful coexistence as well as strength.[71] At diplomatic receptions at the Japanese Embassy in Moscow on November 1 and the Italian Embassy on November 5, several Soviet military officers showed cordiality to Americans and toasted the fact that peace had pre-

69. "For the Triumph of Marxism-Leninism, for Proletarian Internationalism," *Pravda,* November 1, 1962.

70. The most extensive later Kremlinological analysis was Michel Tatu, *Power in the Kremlin: From Khrushchev to Kosygin,* trans. Helen Keitel (New York: Viking Press, 1969; first published in France in 1967), pp. 229–97. See also William Hyland and Richard Wallace Shryock, *The Fall of Khrushchev* (New York: Funk and Wagnalls, 1968), pp. 45–65; and Carl A. Linden, *Khrushchev and the Soviet Leadership, 1957–1964* (Baltimore: Johns Hopkins Press, 1966), pp. 146–73.

The most detailed press analysis, and the exception in treating the whole subject in terms of the context of Soviet-Cuban policy, is Herbert S. Dinerstein, *The Making of a Missile Crisis: October 1962* (Baltimore: Johns Hopkins Press, 1976), pp. 150–229, 239–62.

71. "Speech by Marshal of the Soviet Union R. Ya. Malinovsky," *Pravda,* November 8, 1962. Other key comments by Malinovsky and in the confidential military press evaluating the crisis are discussed later.

vailed. On the other hand, an unidentified "reliable source" told a Western ambassador in Moscow on November 5 that Malinovsky, supported by some civilian leaders, had opposed the withdrawal of the missiles and been overridden. Khrushchev himself was reported to have said the same thing in an informal conversation at a reception. (Khrushchev also acknowledged in conversation at a reception on November 7 that Castro had opposed "his" decision to remove the missiles, and had been told that there was no choice, that *not* to have done so "would have meant war.") And Khrushchev told American editor Norman Cousins several months later that the Soviet military had opposed the missile withdrawal, and had looked at him "as though I was out of my mind or, what was worse, a traitor" for asking if they could guarantee that refusing would not result in a global nuclear war. "So I said to myself," Khrushchev continued, " 'To hell with these maniacs. If I can get the United States to assure me that it will not attempt to overthrow the Cuban government, I will remove the missiles.' "[72]

Finally, an unconfirmed intelligence report stated that when the Supreme Soviet met on December 12, some thirty-five to forty high-ranking military officers who were members absented themselves as a sign of displeasure from the session at which Khrushchev justified his handling of the crisis. If true, that was a significant act of political indiscipline, and the absence of any reports of punitive reaction suggests that Khrushchev at the time was not strong enough to retaliate.

While there is virtually no direct information on the deliberations in Moscow in those critical days, there were some indirect indications in addition to Khrushchev's messages of October 23 and 24 to President Kennedy. In these letters, Khrushchev sought to persuade Kennedy of the legitimacy and peaceful deterrent purpose of the deployments, with no hint of readiness to withdraw the missiles. His message of October 24 opened with a plaintive plea for the president to put himself in Khrushchev's shoes: "Just imagine, Mr. President, that we had presented you with the conditions of an ultimatum which you have presented us by your

72. [Norman Cousins], "The Cuban Missile Crisis: An Anniversary," editorial, *Saturday Review,* vol. 5 (October 15, 1977), p. 4.

action. How would you have reacted to this? I think you would have been indignant at such a step on our part. And this would have been understandable to us."[73]

But actions speak too, and early on the morning of October 24, just as the quarantine took effect, sixteen of the eighteen dry cargo Soviet ships en route and nearing the area were observed to stop dead in the water. Moreover, the five probably carrying missiles and related equipment—including the *Poltava* with the nuclear warheads—soon turned back for the Soviet Union. The Soviet leaders were not prepared to risk running the blockade.

Also on October 24 Khrushchev personally resorted to an unorthodox channel of communication. A visiting American businessman, William E. Knox, was suddenly ushered in for a three-hour meeting with the Soviet leader. Khrushchev admitted the presence of the Soviet missiles—something publicly still denied—and claimed their nuclear warheads were in Cuba, but that the Soviet Union had them under strict control and would never fire nuclear weapons first. Clearly, he wanted to reassure the American leadership on this point. He said that the United States might stop a few ships, but that at some point he would give orders to strike an American blockade ship, or perhaps stop American ships on the high seas somewhere else. Again, he wished both to signal that he would not immediately challenge the quarantine, but that Soviet acquiescence could not be assumed indefinitely. He then raised the matter of the U.S. missiles in Turkey. But rather than proposing a mutual withdrawal, he said that the United States would have to learn to live with the Soviet missiles in Cuba, just as the Soviet Union had learned to live with American missiles in Turkey and elsewhere. Finally, he suggested that perhaps the best way to resolve the crisis would be a personal meeting with President Kennedy in Moscow, or Washington, or perhaps in a rendezvous at sea. Thus it would appear that as of October 24 Khrushchev was

73. This message, and all of the published Khrushchev messages of October 1962, and most subsequent Soviet commentaries to 1982, are conveniently compiled in Ronald R. Pope, ed., *Soviet Views on the Cuban Missile Crisis: Myth and Reality in Foreign Policy Analysis* (Lanham, Md.: University Press of America, 1982); for the quotation, see p. 32.

at least still hoping that the U.S. leadership could be brought to accept the continued presence of Soviet missiles in Cuba.

On October 25, several Soviet diplomats around the world began to break the silence that their initial lack of instructions had imposed.[74] Ambassador Nikita S. Ryzhov in Turkey saw Foreign Minister Feridun Erkin and raised the matter of the Jupiters in Turkey as parallel to Soviet missiles in Cuba, perhaps hinting at a trade, or an implied threat. But several other Soviet envoys began to stress the Soviet desire to end the confrontation peacefully and hinted at readiness to compromise.[75] The one who was most explicit, Ambassador Nikolai A. Mikhailov in Indonesia, told the Indian ambassador there that the Soviet Union would hold off its ships during negotiations and suggested that the removal of the missiles might be negotiable.[76] This message was almost certainly intended to be conveyed to the United States, as it was.

74. Despite an absence of instructions, some Soviet ambassadors—including Dobrynin—in private conversations on October 22 through 24 predicted a stiff Soviet response, such as challenging the quarantine. Ambassador Valerian Zorin at the UN did have instructions—to *deny* the presence of Soviet missiles in Cuba.

75. Among the more unorthodox channels was a London osteopath on the raw edge of British political life. On October 24 Dr. Stephen Ward had lunch with Soviet Naval Attaché Captain Evgeny Ivanov at the latter's invitation and was asked to use his connections to pass along a suggestion that could give Britain a rare opportunity to serve world peace. Ivanov's bait was this: if the British government called a summit conference, Khrushchev would accept and would be ready to turn back Soviet ships and discuss removal of the missiles from Cuba. Ward did pass the message to Sir Harold Caccia, the permanent undersecretary of the Foreign Office, but the idea was not further pursued.

Dr. Ward and Captain Ivanov attained fleeting notoriety some eight months later when Ward's protégée Christine Keeler turned out to share the beds of both Secretary of State for War John Profumo and Captain Ivanov, to the detriment at least of the career of Profumo.

76. Kremlinologists can ponder why Ambassador Mikhailov was chosen to give this "Khrushchev" signal. Nikolai A. Mikhailov was not a career diplomat, having been honorably retired into diplomacy by Khrushchev in 1954. He had been a very senior party leader, one of the secretaries of the Central Committee under Stalin, and for ten years before that, as head of the Komsomol (Communist party youth organization), was the immediate superior of his successor in that position, Aleksandr Shelepin, in October–November 1962 one of the conservative party leaders in the Presidium.

While the signal was made known to the Ex Comm in November 1962,

Little has been disclosed about deliberations within the Soviet leadership, unlike the many memoirs and accounts on the American side. But subsequent Soviet accounts claiming a need for responsible compromise on both sides (discussed later) seem to reflect the balance of judgment reached in Moscow. Whether there were significant arguments over reaching this consensus is not known.

The United States later received information from a reliable Soviet source that the Soviet leadership had decided not to go to war over Cuba even if America invaded, and formalized that decision in a signed top secret Central Committee directive.[77]

As the Soviets often do, even or especially on important matters, they sought to use a deniable and dispensable but trusted Soviet intelligence contact out of official channels to take a sounding and float a trial balloon. On the morning of Friday, October 26, Aleksandr Fomin, officially the Soviet Embassy public affairs counselor (but known to be the KGB *resident,* or station chief), insisted on arranging a lunch meeting with ABC News correspondent John Scali. The story is well known and does not need retelling; through Scali to Secretary Rusk, the Soviets—or, more precisely, whoever in the Soviet leadership Fomin was representing, probably Khrushchev—sounded out a potential deal: Soviet removal of the missiles from Cuba, under UN inspection, in exchange for a U.S. public commitment not to invade Cuba. Rusk's reply, cleared with the White House, was that the United States saw "real possibilities" along the lines suggested, but that "time is very urgent."[78]

That same day UN Secretary General U Thant suggested to Ambassador Adlai Stevenson and John J. McCloy that an American assurance that it would not attack Cuba might be an appropriate quid pro quo for a Soviet withdrawal of its missiles. That suggestion

---

Mikhailov's identity was not noted, and Kremlinologists later poring over the missile crisis have not heretofore known about the unpublicized "Mikhailov signal."

77. This intelligence report, received about six months after the crisis, was both plausible and from a reliable, well-placed source. It has, however, never been either corroborated or disconfirmed by other sources of information.

78. See Hilsman, *To Move a Nation,* pp. 217–19.

may well have been discreetly planted by the Soviets with the secretary general, although we do not have confirming information.

Hours later, about 6:00 P.M., a message was received by the president from Chairman Khrushchev. It bore all the marks of his personal style and appears (from later events) to have been sent without full clearance in the Presidium. Khrushchev proposed that, if the United States would undertake not to invade Cuba (with its own or proxy forces), the reason for the Soviet stationing of the missiles in Cuba would be removed, and the missiles could be withdrawn. While the potential deal was not fully explicit, the message was clear. This was the occasion when Secretary Rusk made his famous remark that we were "eyeball to eyeball, and I think the other fellow just blinked first."

As the president and his Ex Comm advisers were preparing on the morning of the 27th to respond favorably, a second message was received at about 10 o'clock, this time adding a demand for the withdrawal of the American missiles in Turkey. The new message caused extreme concern. The mood became even more grim when, minutes later, word was received that a U-2 reconnaissance plane had been shot down over Cuba and the pilot killed.[79]

_____

79. The reason for the U-2 shoot-down is still not clear. Soviet negotiators in New York blamed it on the Cubans, contending that all antiaircraft systems were in Cuban hands. Khrushchev, on the other hand, had on October 24 told Knox that the antiaircraft surface-to-air (SAM) missiles were securely under Soviet control. U.S. intelligence at the time correctly believed them to have been under Soviet manning and control, although Cubans had been training on the system. The SAM system in October 1962 was in Soviet hands.

Two separate incidents of antiaircraft gunfire at low-flying reconnaissance jets only hours later suggest that it was not an accident or isolated incident. Since the Cubans did control the antiaircraft guns of the Cuban air defense system, they may have been responsible for the latter attacks—although those could have been firings by antiaircraft guns of the Soviet ground combat teams providing protection for the missile sites that were being reconnoitered.

It is possible that the air defense system radars had simply not been able earlier to engage the high-flying U-2s. One problem causing delay in the activation of the SAM system was a deficiency in Cuban high-altitude radar capability, perhaps not fully realized in advance by the Soviet planners. October 27 might just have been the first time the SAM system was able to intercept. That explanation was considered plausible in the intelligence community at the time.

A rather dramatic alternative explanation has been reported by someone with

Moreover, in the next few hours, for the first time two low-level reconnaissance flights were also fired upon, although not hit. It was speculated that Khrushchev might no longer be in control or able to agree to a deal on the basis of the first message. The JCS recommended an air strike and invasion. The State Department proposed a draft message flatly rejecting the Turkish missile trade demanded in the second letter. On the other hand, there was also much discussion that it would be difficult for the administration to make a persuasive case to world opinion, and perhaps to opinion

access to sensitive intelligence, developed some time after the incident (it was not known to intelligence at the time). According to this report, Cuban military forces overran and took over a Soviet-manned SAM site on October 27 and fired the missile that downed the U-2. As noted, Cubans had been training and knew how the SA-2 SAM system operated. This would also be consistent with Cuban antiaircraft gun firings that same day. On the one hand, such a Cuban initiative seems hard to believe. On the other, Castro might have been desperate to head off a feared superpower deal at his expense. This story remains, at this point, unconfirmed.

Another alternative is that someone in the Soviet leadership, necessarily high in the military or able to give an order to the military, was responsible for creating the incident in an unsuccessful attempt to forestall Khrushchev's efforts to arrange a compromise.

An account advanced some years later by a former aide to Castro, Carlos Franqui, held that Fidel Castro himself, while on an inspection visit to a Soviet SAM site, asked how the system operated and how to fire the missiles. When shown, he suddenly fired the missile. See *Time*, March 16, 1981, p. 51. This story, for a number of reasons, including the improbability that the Castro inspection would have coincided with a U-2 flight within range, is implausible and can be dismissed. Castro himself has denied that he fired the missile and has stated that, although he had ordered the antiaircraft gunfire, the Soviets had shot down the U-2 with a SAM missile, without clearing it with the Cubans (who would not, however, have objected). See Jim Hoagland, "Cuba Reconsiders 1962 Understanding: Castro Sheds Light on Downing of U.S. Reconnaissance Plane during Missile Crisis," *Washington Post*, February 3, 1985.

The most bizarre explanation surfaced in the press soon after the crisis (see Arthur J. Olsen, "Chinese Gunners Reported in Cuba," *New York Times*, November 17, 1962) reporting rumors circulating among communist diplomats that *Chinese* military personnel had manned the site and shot down the American plane. In fact, this public rumor was grounded in a secret report by a senior Polish general to a military audience in Warsaw on November 12, 1962, on what he had been told in Moscow. This was transparently a disinformation attempt by Soviet intelligence to fan anti-Chinese sentiment in response to the sharp Chinese attacks on the Soviet handling of the crisis.

Today, after all these years, it is still not clear what authority was responsible for the firing, and for what purpose.

at home as well, that it was worth prolonging or intensifying the crisis rather than accede to withdrawal of obsolete missiles from Turkey. Finally, on the basis of a suggestion by Sorensen and Robert Kennedy, the president decided to respond positively to the first message and simply to ignore the second.[80]

On October 27 the president sent a message to Khrushchev in effect accepting his proposal of October 26. The president had his brother Robert, known to all as his close confidant, also deliver the message through Ambassador Dobrynin and orally give him several additional points. In conveying the message to Dobrynin, Robert Kennedy stressed both the president's readiness to give assurances against an invasion of Cuba and the urgency of a prompt Soviet acceptance. If the *Soviets* did not promptly agree to remove the missiles, " *we* [the United States] would remove them."[81] This was not a bluff. Plans had been set for a possible air strike on Tuesday morning (October 30), although the president had *not* made any final decision, even contingently.

Only some years later did it become known that Robert Kennedy had also, in reply to a question from Dobrynin about the missiles in Turkey, advised him that the stationing of the missiles in Turkey had been a NATO decision, and that the United States could not therefore unilaterally decide to remove them. Disposition of the missiles in Turkey could therefore not be part of a U.S.-Soviet agreement concerning the missiles in Cuba. At the same time, the president had long been thinking of phasing out the missiles from Turkey and Italy, and with an improvement in relations after a resolution of the crisis, the president expected that "within a short time after this crisis was over, those missiles would be gone."[82]

The essential elements of the American proposal of October 27

80. A complete transcript of the October 27 Ex Comm meeting, from a taped recording, has now been declassified and will be published in *International Security,* vol. 12 (forthcoming Winter 1987–88).

Most Ex Comm meetings were not taped, but those held in the Cabinet Room of the White House were. A transcript of the meetings of October 16 has also been declassified and published in *International Security,* vol. 10 (Summer 1985), pp. 164–94.

81. Kennedy, *Thirteen Days,* pp. 103, 108; emphasis added.

82. Ibid., pp. 108–09.

were an *ultimatum* (although Kennedy's account does not indicate so precisely, the Soviets understood they had only some forty-eight to seventy-two hours), *coupled with a way out,* the noninvasion undertaking in exchange for removal of the missiles. In my judgment, the additional sweetener of the private assurance of an American intention to remove the missiles from Turkey and Italy[83] was probably not necessary, although it certainly made it easier for Khrushchev to accept (and to gain his colleagues' acceptance of) the basic over-the-table settlement.[84]

83. On October 29, two days after their key conversation and after Khrushchev's agreement, Dobrynin took an unsigned draft letter to Robert Kennedy. This draft from Khrushchev to the president sought to tie down the U.S. withdrawal of its missiles from Turkey and Italy as part of the deal, seeking a presidential letter to that effect. Robert Kennedy called Dobrynin back the next day, returned the draft Khrushchev letter, and categorically rejected any such written exchange. He informed Dobrynin that if the Soviet Union published anything claiming that there *was* such a deal, the U.S. intentions with respect to the Jupiter missiles would change, and it would negatively reflect on the U.S.-Soviet relationship. See Schlesinger, *Robert Kennedy,* p. 523. The Soviets dropped the matter, and never referred to it in any commentaries until after Robert Kennedy's book revealed the October 27 oral exchange, after which they have been careful to cite that published reference.

Both Kennedy's account and Soviet accounts have made clear that Kennedy's "sweetener" statement was made only after Dobrynin raised the question of the U.S. Jupiter missiles in Turkey, as had Khrushchev's October 27 letter, and also that Kennedy's statement about the American administration's intentions was the first to refer to the Jupiters in Italy as well as those in Turkey, because the American plans to phase the system out applied to the deployments in both countries. Not mentioned in Kennedy's book, in response to a question from Dobrynin on October 27, he suggested the missiles would probably be gone in four or five months.

Immediately after the crisis, the United States moved within the alliance to take the missiles out of Italy and Turkey, and they were gone by April 25, 1963, less than six months later.

84. A recent Soviet account correctly describes the implied threat and offer for a noninvasion pledge in exchange for removal of the missiles and the president's stated intention with respect to the missiles in Turkey and Italy, which it describes as a "supplementary promise." See A. A. Kokoshin and S. M. Rogov, *Serye kardinaly belogo doma* (Grey Cardinals of the White House) (Moscow: Novosti, 1986), pp. 60–62.

On the ultimative element, this account states that in addition to Robert Kennedy's representation, "the Soviet government received information [intelligence] that an attack on Cuba could take place in the next two or three

The hours between the president's message of October 27 and the Soviet reply the next morning were extremely tense in Washington (and no doubt in Moscow too). This was the day called "Black Saturday" because of the disappointment and deep concern after the second Khrushchev message. Although the information did not reach the Ex Comm, there was a report that the Soviet Embassy in Washington had started to burn its records, a precautionary measure if diplomatic relations were going to be suddenly severed. And in Moscow for the first time "popular" demonstrations were mounted in front of the U.S. Embassy. Was Khrushchev still in charge, and could he now accept the deal he himself had proposed? Also on October 27–28 communists in Venezuela, heeding a public call from Castro, bombed four U.S. oil company power stations in the Lake Maracaibo region. While not controlled by Moscow, and probably not by Havana either, this action added to the sense of tension in the Ex Comm.[85]

Another incident that contributed to the tension was an unintended American military action. On October 27 a U-2 reconnaissance plane, apparently on a routine air-sampling nuclear detection mission, strayed over the Chukhotsk peninsula in northeastern Siberia and caused a local Soviet air defense reaction. The pilot had made a navigational error and returned to Alaska without incident. President Kennedy, when told of it, broke the tension with a laugh and comment, "There is always some so-and-so [sonofabitch] who doesn't get the word."[86]

---

days." Ibid., pp. 60–61. The first Soviet reference to "reports" (in the plural) of an expected attack in two or three days was in Khrushchev's speech of December 12, 1962.

85. Under the circumstances, even quite innocent events were cause for concern. On October 27 a Soviet transport plane was permitted to fly through Dakar for Brazil. It was feared in Washington that the plane would go to Havana, despite its flight plan, and might have nuclear weapons aboard. In fact it did fly to Rio de Janeiro as declared, to take home the body of the Soviet ambassador to Brazil, who had perished in a drowning accident.

86. See Hilsman, *To Move a Nation*, p. 221.

One incident that fortunately did *not* happen and has not been reported deserves mention. A day or two before the U-2 incident, a member of the Ex Comm in his other duties by chance became aware of another routine on-going operation that should have been reconsidered under crisis conditions. A U.S.

Moscow probably saw the U-2 intrusion as yet another crass American reminder of its strategic superiority. The location of the incident argued against its being taken as a serious military reconnaissance mission of the type that might be made on the eve of hostilities.

Khrushchev complained about the overflight in his next message, asking if it were a "provocation," happening "at a time as troubled as the one through which we are passing, when everything has been put into combat readiness." Kennedy expressed "regret" for the intrusion by the unarmed plane, attributed it to a serious navigational error by the pilot, and said he would "see to it that every precaution is taken to prevent recurrence." The next day a standdown of all U-2 flights around the Soviet Union was ordered.

Rusk arranged for Scali to contact Fomin again and give him hell for the "double cross" of the Soviet step back in the second message, which threatened to drive the crisis again to a dangerous point. Fomin's message to Moscow after this second conversation reinforced Khrushchev's arguments to accept the American proposal, as Fomin later told Scali.[87]

According to a senior Soviet diplomat, Khrushchev personally told him that the United States was ready on October 27 to invade Cuba, and that he decided to pull the missiles out of Cuba because a communist Cuba without missiles was better for Soviet interests than a U.S.-occupied Cuba. While not confirmed, this account is very plausible.[88] It also accords with other information as to the Soviet decision.

The Soviet leaders agreed to the president's proposal, or rather

---

intelligence-collection ship for intercepting communications was perilously close to Cuban waters. No one had remembered it until then; it was promptly ordered to move a safe distance away. No incident occurred. There is a strong tendency not to learn lessons from near-misses; in 1967 a similar ship in a similar situation, the *Liberty*, was attacked by Israeli aircraft and ships, and in 1968 its sister-ship, the *Pueblo*, was captured by the North Koreans.

87. Ibid., pp. 222–24.

88. The statement was made privately by a Soviet ambassador accredited to a Western European country on October 31, 1962, and was promptly learned of by the United States. It is difficult to see how it would have been in Soviet interest to invent this statement for disinformation.

to his acceptance of the first Khrushchev proposal, the next day, and publicly broadcast the fact.[89] President Kennedy in turn issued a statement welcoming Khrushchev's "statesmanlike" decision to withdraw the missiles (omitting to mention that part of the deal was an American pledge of noninvasion of Cuba). On October 28 the crisis was essentially resolved.[90]

From the Soviet (and Cuban) standpoint, the United States had made a major concession. If one believed that the United States had been intending to invade Cuba, an American pledge under the circumstances was an important step. On the other hand, if the U.S. leadership was not planning an invasion, a pledge of restraint was no real sacrifice, while obtaining the removal of the Soviet missiles *was* important, for domestic political, international political, and military reasons. Within the U.S. leadership, there was no real debate over acceptance of a noninvasion commitment. There had been those who favored an air strike and invasion in order to remove both the missiles and Castro, but once the alternative of removing the missiles without resort to force was a real choice, *no one* in the Ex Comm argued for invading or even keeping an invasion option.[91]

89. The reply was broadcast on Radio Moscow at 9:00 A.M. Washington time), about two hours before the official copy was received. The Soviet leaders were taking no chances on a delay that might see an American military move. Khrushchev's letter of October 26 had experienced a long delay in transmission to Washington from the U.S. Embassy in Moscow.

90. The Soviets moved promptly to begin dismantling the missile facilities, without even waiting for a response from Kennedy confirming agreement. Orders were received in Havana that afternoon, and observable work on dismantling began within two hours. Inexplicably, at one site *construction* continued the next day, before work there also shifted to dismantling; someone just didn't get the word (or couldn't believe it). The dismantling was thorough; everything that could not be taken away was broken up and bulldozed.

91. This consensus included of course Secretary of Defense McNamara, who had consistently opposed an air strike or invasion, and also General Maxwell Taylor, the chairman of the JCS and only military man on the Ex Comm, who had earlier argued for an air strike and invasion. A few senior military men, notably General Curtis LeMay of the U.S. Air Force, continued to argue for an air strike on October 27 (and even on October 28!), and Admiral George Anderson, the chief of naval operations, complained that "we had been had." But these were a minority even among the military leaders. The strongest civilian advocate

What would have happened if the Soviet government had not agreed on October 28? If it had narrowed the possibilities for negotiation and insisted that the missiles would stay, the United States might well eventually have attacked the missile bases, followed by an invasion. If it had agreed to remove its missiles from Cuba, but insisted on a formal U.S. pledge to remove American missiles from Turkey, a diplomatic solution could probably have been found. But the risks were high.

No one can be absolutely certain what President Kennedy would have done if Khrushchev had rejected his proposal of October 27 and defied his tacit ultimatum. At the time, I and many others on the Ex Comm or working closely with it believed he would have ordered an air strike. Others, however, including Robert Mc-Namara, believed he would have tightened the quarantine by including petroleum, and perhaps taken other steps short of direct military action, while continuing to negotiate. Some of his closest advisers, Theodore Sorensen and Arthur Schlesinger, believed he would have made further concessions, including if necessary an outright deal trading our missiles in Turkey for the Soviet missiles in Cuba. It should be recalled that in 1962, and indeed until 1969, most members of the Ex Comm and all others except a handful of close advisers of the president knew nothing of the unilateral "sweetener" in Robert Kennedy's statement to Dobrynin of American intentions to phase out the missiles in Turkey and Italy.

Startling new information revealed recently by Dean Rusk makes it appear highly likely that President Kennedy would not have launched an air strike, and would have continued negotiations. Disclosed only recently by Secretary Rusk, it now is known that on October 27, after sending Robert Kennedy to deliver the key message to Dobrynin, President Kennedy privately asked Rusk to call the late Andrew Cordier, the former deputy UN secretary general then at Columbia University, and ask him to be prepared

---

of an attack on the missiles in the early days of the crisis, Dean Acheson, no longer served as an adviser after October 20, but even he congratulated the president after the outcome. CIA Director John McCone, a consistent advocate of military action during the thirteen days, was reluctant to give up the objective of removing Castro, and was probably the Ex Comm member most disinclined to have the United States accept a commitment against invasion.

to suggest to Secretary General U Thant that he propose to both the Soviet Union and the United States that they remove their missiles respectively from Cuba and Turkey. He was given a precise message to this effect, but told not to actually make the suggestion until receiving a signal from Rusk (after a possible later decision by the president). Thus President Kennedy wanted to have in ready reserve a neutral request to which he could respond favorably much more easily than he could to a Soviet demand. While the whole question was rendered moot by Khrushchev's acceptance of the president's October 27 proposal, it is clear that Kennedy was more inclined to pursue additional negotiations and even to accept a compromise involving an explicit commitment to withdrawal of U.S. missiles from Turkey in conjunction with withdrawal of the Soviet missiles from Cuba rather than resort to a military attack on Cuba.[92]

I believe that both the U.S. and Soviet leaderships reached a sensible and statesmanlike compromise resolution of the problem.

92. This disclosure was made in a letter from Dean Rusk to James G. Blight, February 25, 1987. See Lukas, *New York Times Magazine,* August 30, 1987, p. 58; and James G. Blight, Joseph S. Nye, Jr., and David A. Welch, "The Cuban Missile Crisis Revisited," *Foreign Affairs,* vol. 66 (Fall 1987), pp. 178–79.

The Settlement

THERE WAS widespread relief and near euphoria over the successful conclusion of the crisis among the U.S. leaders and people, and among the Soviet leaders and people as well. Nonetheless, while the October 28 agreement was crucial, it did *not* end the crisis. Several issues remained or arose in the next three weeks requiring resolution, and there remained the need to implement the agreed terms. Intense and difficult negotiations were required to convert the October 27–28 exchange of messages into practice. One issue was the question of weapons that the United States considered "offensive" other than the missiles—principally, the IL-28 light bombers. Another was the question of inspection arrangements to assure the withdrawal of the missiles and dismantling of the launch facilities. A third was the question of means to provide assurance against future reintroduction of offensive arms. A fourth was the form and content of U.S. assurances against invasion of Cuba. And finally, only with resolution at least of the issue of which "offensive" weapons would be removed, and verification of the removal of the missiles, was the United States prepared to end the quarantine. This phase of the crisis lasted from October 28 to November 20. Indeed, in one important respect—an American assurance against invasion of Cuba—the final phase continued inconclusively until mid-January 1963, and was left in uncertainty for much longer.

Meanwhile, the United States placed heavy reliance on extensive aerial reconnaissance—a unilateral impingement on Cuban sovereignty not covered in the agreement resolving the crisis.[93]

93. Aerial reconnaissance of Cuba by the United States had been conducted ever since October 1960, on an average of about two flights a month before the

While the Soviets raised only pro forma objections, there was considerable concern over what the Cubans might do—concern even on the part of the Soviets.[94]

One of the early potential dangers, then, was possible Cuban attack on American reconnaissance aircraft. The fifth appended memorandum to this study, drafted on November 5, called for tit-for-tat reprisal to any attack (in practice, probably only in response to any successful attack) on overflying American aircraft.[95] This memorandum was written mainly to counter calls for restraint on the grounds that the U.S.-Soviet crisis could be reignited if Soviet personnel were killed in such American reprisal attacks. Concern over Soviet reaction to Russian casualties had been introduced into the crisis debates as early as October 16 by Ambassadors Thompson and Bohlen. It was a valid point. Nonetheless, many of us regarded it as a factor that should not be permitted to exclude consideration of options. It had remained a factor weighed variously, along with others, by different members of the Ex Comm throughout the debate on an air strike. Now the question arose again, in a more limited way, in connection with consideration of contingency responses to the shooting down of another American reconnaissance plane. President Kennedy had overruled such reprisal when Major Rudolf Anderson, Jr., was shot down at the height of the crisis on October 27.[96] If another aircraft had been

---

heavy military buildup of August to October 1962. It continued after the missile crisis until early 1977, when President Jimmy Carter ended it as a gesture toward normalizing relations with Cuba.

94. In his letter of October 27, in addition to protesting the accidental U-2 overflight of the USSR that day (and recalling the earlier one of August 30), Khrushchev also urged Kennedy "to bear in mind that a violation of Cuban air space by American aircraft may also have dangerous consequences." N. Khrushchev, "A Message from the Chairman of the Council of Ministers of the USSR to the President of the United States and the General Secretary of the U.N.," *Vneshnayaya politika, 1962,* p. 424. In addition, on October 30, First Deputy Foreign Minister Vasily Kuznetsov (in a discussion with Stevenson) urged that the United States limit itself to peripheral flights and oblique reconnaissance photography. As further insurance, the Soviets did not turn over control of the SAM sites to the Cubans until many months later.

95. See Appendix document E.

96. The president's decision became known at the operating level in the

shot down after the crisis had been essentially resolved, I am sure he would also have held back in the first instance. If the threat of continued air defense interference had threatened our ability to verify the removal and continuing absence of the missiles, however, it would have been necessary to assure continuing air reconnaissance. A tentative decision was made by the president on November 8 calling for careful examination of the particular circumstances in any incident, and for a presidential message to Khrushchev explaining the rationale for our limited military response, but endorsing the concept of measured retaliation that some of us had advocated.[97]

The president sent John McCloy to New York to work with Ambassador Adlai Stevenson on the American side as leaders of a bipartisan team that also included Undersecretary of State Ball and Deputy Secretary of Defense Roswell Gilpatric. The Soviet government sent First Deputy Foreign Minister Vasily Kuznetsov to work with Ambassador Valerian Zorin. And, most important, on November 1 the Presidium sent First Deputy Chairman of the Council of Ministers Anastas Mikoyan to Havana to negotiate with Fidel Castro about the Cuban role in the settlement, and more generally to discuss Soviet-Cuban relations under the new circumstances.

Mikoyan's task was formidable. Castro was furious at the Soviet leadership for pressuring him to accept the missiles and then agreeing—without consulting him—to remove them. He had been told the missiles would be a valuable sign of the Soviet commitment, in one sense a substitute for the Warsaw Pact alliance membership he had sought and been denied. And now they were being removed at the demand of his enemy.

Cuban troops took up positions around the four Soviet missile bases on October 28 and remained there for three days (at one site

---

Pentagon barely in time to prevent a planned air strike on the probable offending air defense missile site that was about to be made in accordance with earlier-approved contingency plans.

97. See "Memorandum for the NSC Executive Committee: Revised Course of Action in the Contingency that a Surveillance Plane Is Shot at or Destroyed," November 8, 1962 (Top Secret; now declassified).

reportedly until November 3, after Mikoyan arrived). This fact was not immediately known, but was soon learned by the United States. It has never before been disclosed.

Mikoyan was the only Soviet Presidium member to have visited Cuba (in February 1960), even before the Soviet Union and Cuba had established diplomatic relations on May 8, 1960. Mikoyan had negotiated economic and trade agreements then that helped Castro to wean Cuba away from economic dependence on the United States. The Soviet leadership hoped the same means would again help to mollify Castro. Mikoyan was accompanied by Artemy A. Alikhanov, deputy chairman of the State Committee for Foreign Economic Relations, in charge of aid and trade. But while that did help, it certainly did not solve Mikoyan's problems.

Mikoyan was in Havana for twenty-two days. It took him sixteen days to obtain Castro's reluctant agreement to give up the IL-28 bombers. He was unable to secure Castro's acquiescence to any external inspection and verification measures in Cuba, and in turn the Soviet Union was unable to get from the United States formal assurances against invasion of Cuba to still Castro's abiding mistrust of American promises on that score.

Castro also sought to establish his own terms for any resolution of relations with the United States. Immediately after the public exchange of Khrushchev's and Kennedy's messages on October 28, Castro set forth in a letter to UN Secretary General U Thant, made public, his own five conditions. Castro demanded a cessation of the economic blockade imposed earlier by the United States, a cessation of all covert sabotage, subversion, and infiltration operations carried out by the United States and accomplices, an end to "piratical raids being carried out from bases in the United States and Puerto Rico," cessation of U.S. air intrusions, and U.S. withdrawal from and return to Cuba of the naval base at Guantánamo Bay.[98] Mikoyan and the Soviet leaders had no choice but to endorse publicly the justice of Castro's demands, while seeking in practice to steer toward a realistic settlement.

98. Letter, Fidel Castro to U Thant, UN General Assembly Document A/5271, October 28, 1962, pp. 1–2; reprinted in Larson, ed., *"Cuban Crisis" of 1962*, 2d ed., pp. 197–98.

Castro was adamant against the idea of international inspection of any kind in Cuba. The Soviets nonetheless dismantled the sites, destroying what could not be removed, and cooperatively displayed the missiles as they were removed on the decks of Soviet cargo ships to facilitate American observation. This outcome, while satisfactory for the time, did not provide ironclad assurances for the future, and led the United States to hold back from a firm noninvasion commitment of the kind envisaged on October 28.

The major issue holding up an end to the quarantine and to the military alert was the U.S. insistence that the "offensive weapons" mentioned by President Kennedy in his September warnings and October 23 quarantine proclamation included bomber aircraft, and Soviet and Cuban objection to removal of the forty-two IL-28 jet light bombers.[99] At first the Soviet negotiators believed this to be a minor matter, but they soon realized that the United States was serious in insisting on inclusion of the bombers. The fact that the *Soviet* proposals had referred to "the weapons that you [the United States] consider 'offensive,'" rather than mentioning missiles, weakened the Soviet case.

There were divided views among American policymakers and advisers over how strongly to stand on this issue. Some believed it was unwise and imprudent to appear to be pushing our advantage by raising an issue over the IL-28s or any other weapon system. Some wished to press our advantage and demand the removal of all Soviet military forces. Others believed we should seek removal at least of the IL-28 bombers.[100]

While the administration had been prepared until October 16 to

99. The Ilyushin-28 jet light bomber was already more than a dozen years old at the time. It had been virtually removed from active service in the Soviet Air Force in 1960. Still, it could carry 6,000 pounds of bombload 600 nautical miles (or less weight to 750 nautical miles) operational radius, and it could be a step toward increasing offensive capabilities. Even when it was a Soviet bomber, during the 1950s, it was not actually given a nuclear delivery role, although that fact was not appreciated by most American military analysts in 1962, since it had always been credited as having a "potential" for nuclear delivery—as, of course, do civilian airliners.

100. The following discussion draws heavily on my article "American Reaction to Soviet Aircraft in Cuba, 1962 and 1978," *Political Science Quarterly,* vol. 95 (Fall 1980), pp. 427–39.

accept some jet light bombers in Cuba, as clearly indicated in McGeorge Bundy's earlier-cited statement of October 14, once the Soviets were known to be introducing long-range nuclear-armed ballistic missiles, it had been considered necessary to draw more tightly the definition of unacceptable offensive arms in Cuba.[101]

On October 22 the president had applied the quarantine to "all offensive military equipment" going to Cuba. After describing the MRBM and IRBM missile sites, he stated: "In addition, jet bombers, capable of carrying nuclear weapons, are now being uncrated and assembled in Cuba, while the necessary air bases are being prepared." The quarantine order itself, of October 23,

101. When on Sunday, October 14, McGeorge Bundy had appeared on ABC's "Issues and Answers" and been asked about charges by Senator Keating that the Soviets were installing strategic missiles in Cuba, he expressed strong doubt that the Soviets and Cubans would "attempt to install a major offensive capability" in Cuba, and stated flatly that "I *know* there is no present evidence" that they are doing so. He also addressed in some detail the matter of aircraft. "It is true," he said, "that the MiG fighters which have been put in Cuba for more than a year now, and any possible additions in the form of aircraft, might have a certain marginal capability for moving against the United States. But I think we have to bear in mind the relative magnitudes. . . . So far, everything that has been delivered in Cuba falls within the categories of aid which the Soviet Union has provided, for example, to neutral states like Egypt or Indonesia, and I should not be surprised to see additional military assistance of this sort." See Hilsman, *To Move a Nation,* p. 180. Almost literally at the same time Bundy was speaking, the U-2 was overflying Cuba and obtaining the first clear evidence of the construction of medium-range ballistic missiles in Cuba. It also confirmed that crates observed arriving in Cuba on September 28 did, indeed, as suspected contain IL-28 jet light bombers.

On October 10 U.S. Navy reconnaissance photos of Soviet ships approaching Cuba—photos actually taken on September 28, but unaccountably only circulated in Washington on October 9–10—showed topside storage of crates that intelligence analysts quickly identified as probably containing disassembled IL-28 light bombers. This was the first indication that the bombers were being provided to Cuba. The suspect IL-28 crates, together with the unconfirmed reports and suspicions of offensive missiles and the continuing SAM deployments, had led to scheduling the October 14 U-2 photo reconnaissance mission, which observed the crates and the beginning of aircraft assembly at two airfields.

Bundy had anticipated the IL-28s, and his statement on October 14 clearly signaled that a modest number of these bombers for conventional bomb delivery— earlier supplied both to Egypt and Indonesia—would not, alone, be regarded by the administration as representing a "major offensive capability." But of course after October 16 it was not Ilyushins alone—the MRBMs and IRBMs had *not* been expected and they *did* represent a major offensive capability. The line was redrawn to seek the exclusion of all surface-to-surface missiles and all bombers.

included "bomber aircraft" among the offensive arms prohibited from entering Cuba.

During the six days of confrontation, from October 22 to 28, there were no other references to the IL-28s or more generally to aircraft, although President Kennedy did refer in his letter to Khrushchev of October 22 to removing both "long-range missile bases" and "other offensive weapon systems in Cuba" (not specified), and in his letter of October 27 he referred to "all weapon systems in Cuba capable of offensive use." Khrushchev, for his part, referred on October 28 to "the weapons you describe as offensive," in agreeing to their removal.

On October 28, at the tenth Ex Comm meeting, the issue arose. The president stated that offensive weapons "in our view" included the IL-28 bombers, but that "we should not get 'hung up' on the IL-28 bombers." The president was prepared for the U.S. side to argue to the Soviets that the IL-28s were among the weapons *we* viewed as "offensive," and therefore were covered by the convenient circumlocution used by Khrushchev. But he was not comfortable with the fact that virtually the whole crisis exchange had focused on the missiles; in the record of the meeting the president's words were paraphrased as stating that "he did not want to get into a position where we would appear to be going back on our part of the deal. The IL-28 bombers were less important than the strategic missiles."[102] This somewhat equivocal stand was, of course, known only to those most directly involved in the crisis management. And the decision did not specify how far to press the issue, if the Soviets were adamant, before deciding we were stymied.

Following the Ex Comm meeting, I was tasked at the State Department with preparing a paper on the subject. I submitted a memorandum titled "Considerations in Defining Weapons which Must Be Removed from Cuba," to Deputy Undersecretary U. Alexis Johnson on October 29, and he in turn cabled it to Undersecretary Ball in New York. In the memorandum, I noted that "we would like to see the maximum military withdrawal from Cuba, but we must balance against this a reasonable interpretation of what is intolerable to us." For example, the president had clearly

102. "Summary Record of NSC Executive Committee Meeting No. 10, October 28, 1962, 11:10 A.M.," p. 2 (Top Secret; now declassified).

indicated on September 4 that the weapons then in Cuba—including the MiG fighters, coastal defense cruise missiles, and missile-armed patrol boats—were not then regarded as "offensive." On the other hand, the quarantine had included the bombers. I concluded that in addition to the missiles, the IL-28 jet light bombers (and the warheads and supporting equipment for those missile and bomber systems) must also be included.[103]

On November 1 the president authorized immediate low-level reconnaissance flights both over the missile sites, to check on the dismantling, and over the IL-28 airfields. "The major reason for overflying the IL-28s," as stated in the record of the Ex Comm meeting, "is to make clear that we consider these planes 'offensive weapons' to be removed by the Russians, and, therefore, we must know whether they are being dismantled."[104]

On November 2 reconnaissance photos taken the previous day showed continued assembly of the IL-28s, as well as continued dismantling of the MRBM and IRBM sites.[105]

On November 2 the matter was considered at Ex Comm Meeting no. 17, and the president made his decision: the IL-28s must be removed. The other short-range tactical systems, and Soviet military personnel, were not included. The president on November 3 issued instructions including a "requirement" for removal of "all bombers and their equipment," as well as all offensive missiles and equipment. He stated, "All Americans should stick firmly to this position."[106]

Direct negotiations with the Soviets, apart from the Kennedy-Khrushchev correspondence, were centered in New York, where

103. I have not appended the available text of the memorandum because extensive deletions in declassification, made in the period of U.S. government sensitivity over MiG-23s in Cuba, eviscerate the substance.

104. "NSC Executive Committee Record of Action, November 1, 1962, 10:00 A.M., Meeting No. 16," p. 1 (Top Secret; now declassified).

105. Assembly of IL-28s continued after October 28. During the first half of November a curious discrepancy was observed; at one of the two airfields where crated IL-28s were located, Holguín, assembly of aircraft soon stopped, while at the other, San Julian, it continued up until the final decision on November 19.

106. Telegram no. 1189, State Department to the U.S. Mission to the United Nations, November 3, 1962, p. 2 (Top Secret; now declassified). (Hereafter State to USUN.)

Stevenson and McCloy had begun meeting with Mikoyan and Kuznetsov on October 29. Following the Ex Comm meeting on October 28 and the cabling of my memorandum on October 29 to New York, Stevenson was instructed to provide to the Soviets the "list of weapons deemed offensive by the United States," including "bomber aircraft" and "bombs, air-to-surface rockets and guided missiles." In a dinner meeting of Stevenson and McCloy with Mikoyan and Kuznetsov on November 1, dealing with many matters, the Americans *forgot* to give the Soviets the list! Stevenson remedied this by a letter to Mikoyan the next day, November 2. Apart from thanking Mikoyan for the dinner, the letter read in full: "One thing that Mr. McCloy and I neglected to discuss with you last night was the list of items that the United States considers in the category of offensive weapons within the meaning of the exchange between President Kennedy and Chairman Khrushchev. Such a list is appended to this letter. We trust that the weapons you plan to remove include all those on this list."[107]

Reinforced by the president's firm instructions of November 3, Stevenson specifically raised the issue of the IL-28s with Kuznetsov on that same day, noting the continued assembly of the bombers and stating that they should be removed.[108] On November 5 UN Secretary General U Thant also raised the issue of the IL-28s with Kuznetsov, who argued that the question of the bombers was "a new issue" and had not been "covered" in the Kennedy-Khrushchev correspondence.[109] That same day Robert Kennedy met with Ambassador Dobrynin and told him that "it was very clear that the bombers, the IL-28s, had to go."[110] On November 6, the president communicated directly to Khrushchev his insistence that the bombers be removed.[111] On November 7, Secretary Rusk cabled

107. Letter, Adlai Stevenson to Anastas Mikoyan, November 2, 1962.

108. Telegram no. 1625, USUN to State, November 3, 1962, p. 1 (Secret; now declassified).

109. Telegram no. 1635, USUN to State, November 5, 1962, p. 3 (Secret; now declassified).

110. Robert Kennedy, memorandum of conversation with Ambassador Anatoly Dobrynin, November 5, 1962.

111. Letter, President John F. Kennedy to Chairman Nikita S. Khrushchev, November 6, 1962.

Stevenson: "Our primary purpose is to get the MRBMs and IL-28 bombers out, and we would go far in reducing our list of offensive weapons in order to achieve this purpose." On November 8 and 13, Stevenson and McCloy met again with Kuznetsov and Zorin in continued difficult arguments over the IL-28s (as well as over the establishment of adequate inspection in Cuba and verification of withdrawal of the missile systems, which had been at issue since the negotiations in New York had begun).

This was the situation Mikoyan faced in Cuba. The IL-28s posed a special difficulty for the Soviets. Unlike the missile systems, which remained exclusively in Soviet hands at all times and would have continued to do so indefinitely, the IL-28s were to be transferred to the Cubans, as had the MiGs and other arms supplied. The Soviets did not, in fact, regard them as part of their own offensive forces and did not intend to provide them with nuclear delivery capabilities. They naturally did not wish to renege on their earlier commitment to provide them to the Cubans. In the discussions in New York they repeatedly stressed that the aircraft now belonged to Cuba and could not be withdrawn without Cuban authorization (although, to allay our concerns, they did state the bombers were still physically under Soviet control). The Cubans, understandably, were even more adamant. The United States, however, was determined and pressed the issue.

This distinction in the status of the IL-28s presented something of a problem for the United States, too, although it was not given much weight except in terms of recognizing a possible difficulty in marshalling support of world opinion if the Cubans and Soviets were adamant and we continued to press the issue. Most, if not all, members of the Ex Comm considered our position justified. At the same time, as Bundy had mentioned publicly on October 14, IL-28s had been transferred to Egypt and Indonesia, and the United States and world community had not regarded that as other than normal and acceptable military assistance.

Strong feelings were generated and expressed by various of those involved in advising the president on what to do about the IL-28 bombers (and the other issues still unresolved, including verification).

There tended to be replays of the debates that had taken place in the first week of the crisis, and again in the second, between the three schools: to resort if necessary to military action to eliminate the bombers, to tighten the quarantine to include petroleum, or to concede on the issue. By and large the same people held to the same positions. The main difference was a much stronger readiness to consider conceding on this issue. Some believed that we had won on the main issue, the Soviet withdrawal of the missiles, and should not press our luck in forcing Moscow to back down again.

I recall an argument I had with a senior State Department official in early November, in which he challenged me as to the difference between IL-28s in Cuba and, say, in Indonesia. My first reply was that from Cuba they could strike Oak Ridge, which they could not from Java; but that was only a debater's argument. The real point was, as I argued, that the president had publicly committed us to regard the IL-28s as part and parcel of a dangerous offensive arms buildup in Cuba in his quarantine speech of October 22, and that was why the IL-28s as well as the missiles must come out. While the MiG-21s might be just as dangerous in potential, and while both the Ilyushins and MiGs in fact represented no real threat so long as not armed with nuclear weapons, nonetheless the United States had committed itself to regard the Ilyushin "bombers" as dangerous, and had not so committed itself with respect to MiG fighter-bombers. I felt that difference was crucial, as I had argued in my memorandum of October 29, and as the president had decided on November 2.

At several meetings in mid-November, in particular on November 12 and 16, the Ex Comm debated this subject. Sentiment was strong for threatening Khrushchev privately with a stiffer blockade if he would not agree. McNamara and Bundy favored a stiffer blockade. General Taylor, speaking for the Joint Chiefs of Staff, recommended bombing the Cuban airfields. He was supported by Treasury Secretary Douglas Dillon. The extent of hardening resolve was reflected in a State Department contingency paper of November 14, based on the preceding Ex Comm discussion, proposing a range of action including not only "tightening of the blockade" (we did not always bother with the euphemism "quarantine"), but also such measures as " 'harassing surveillance' from the air," going beyond necessary reconnaissance. The paper suggested: "Up to a point this surveillance can be intensified as a measure of psychological warfare. But using aerial reconnaissance as a means of provoking attack on our planes, which would in turn justify retaliation from the air on Cuban targets (including the IL-28's on the ground), is not regarded as an appropriate form of action, *at least until all of the above steps have been played out.*"[112]

An IL-28 crisis thus threatened to follow hard on the heels of the missile crisis. Personally, from indications at the time, I believe that if the Soviets had said they would not remove the aircraft, President Kennedy would have expanded the "quarantine"; I am sure that he would not have taken the JCS recommendation in that contingency "to take them [the IL-28s] out by air attack."

The Soviet negotiators in New York finally offered to remove the planes quietly *after* the United States ended the blockade and made its "no-invasion" pledge; presumably Moscow felt that with this much of an American concession they could force Castro's acceptance and save face for the USSR.[113] But the American negotiators insisted on withdrawal of the bombers before an end to the quarantine, and noted that the no-invasion pledge involved other unsettled issues as well, mainly on-site verification in Cuba that no offensive weapons remained or would be reintroduced.

On November 18, McCloy told Kuznetsov (who had complained that the United States was "stalling" in the negotiations) that the president was scheduling a press conference for 6:00 P.M. on November 20, and that the Soviets must promise before that time

112. "Cuban Contingency Paper: Next Steps on the IL-28s," memorandum from Deputy Undersecretary of State U. Alexis Johnson to McGeorge Bundy, with copies to all Ex Comm members, November 14, 1962, pp. 2–3; emphasis added.

I participated in the drafting of this paper for the Ex Comm. I believed we should press hard for removal of the IL-28s and I was confident the Soviets would eventually find some way to accede. I did not believe we should resort to an air attack on the airfields.

113. Telegram no. 1856, USUN to State, November 19, 1962, p. 7 (Top Secret; now declassified).

to withdraw the IL-28 bombers, or "it will put in question whether in fact we have an agreement with [the] Soviet Union in regard to removal of offensive weapons from Cuba."[114] On November 19 the United States informed its NATO and OAS allies at the head of government or foreign minister level that the Soviets had not yet agreed to remove the bombers and that unspecified further measures, by implication a tightened quarantine, might be required. In addition, the president sent personal messages to President Charles de Gaulle, Chancellor Konrad Adenauer, and Prime Minister Harold Macmillan advising them that the United States might have to resort to "renewed action" and expressing appreciation for their "firm support."[115]

On November 19 Castro gave in on the Ilyushins (although not on inspection issues). Early on November 20 Khrushchev informed the president and promised that the IL-28s would be removed within thirty days. He still objected that in the October exchange of key letters Kennedy had not made "a single mention of bomber aircraft," and that the IL-28s were obsolete and "at present cannot be classified as offensive types of weapons." But he agreed to withdraw them in exchange for American lifting of the quarantine.[116] That same day the president lifted the quarantine. All the missiles had by then been withdrawn.

In his press conference on November 20, the president announced that the Soviets had agreed to remove the bombers, and that the quarantine would be lifted. The SAC alert was cancelled. On November 21 the USSR and Warsaw Pact nominal alerts were, in turn, cancelled. The bombers were removed on December 6–7. On December 12 Khrushchev informed the Supreme Soviet that the missiles and the IL-28s had been withdrawn, in exchange for an American promise not to invade Cuba.

Once the missiles were being taken out, American attention had focused principally on the IL-28s. There were, however, three additional elements in the American position with respect to

114. Ibid., p. 4. This message reported on the discussion of November 18.

115. Telegram no. 939, State circular, November 19, 1962, pp. 3–4 (Secret; now declassified).

116. Letter, Nikita S. Khrushchev to John F. Kennedy, November 20, 1962.

weapons to be dealt with. One was the removal of nuclear warheads in Cuba (if any); another was assurance against a Soviet submarine base; and third was a less clear-cut but growing interest in seeking Soviet withdrawal of their ground combat forces.

There was no real issue over the withdrawal of nuclear warheads. The United States had included "warheads" for missiles and bombers in the list Stevenson had given to Mikoyan on November 2. On November 5 a message was sent to Stevenson and McCloy in the name of the president, mainly on the IL-28s, but also stating that "we need assurances on warheads as much as on missiles themselves. Moreover, we need to know about possible warheads for IL-28s and even MiG 21s."[117] A later listing given on November 8 specified missiles, bombers, and "any nuclear warheads for missiles, nuclear bombs for aircraft, or any type nuclear weapon."[118] Even before that renewed instruction, however, Kuznetsov on November 6 had said the question of removal of nuclear warheads was "a detail," that no doubt warheads would be removed "if indeed any warheads are in Cuba"; the Soviet Union was removing "everything" associated with the so-called offensive missiles. Later the Soviets gave categorical assurances to that effect. On November 18 Kuznetsov told McCloy that "he was now authorized to say that no nuclear weapons whatsoever were any longer on the territory of Cuba," and that the Soviet government reaffirmed that "all nuclear weapons had been removed and that they were not going to reintroduce them."[119] While couched in terms that implied that there had been warheads in Cuba, the Soviet purpose was to reassure the United States—which had raised the issue as though there had been. The Soviets did not want to stimulate American suspicions or a new issue by stating that there never had been any on the island, even if there had not.

The United States did not want to admit that it did not know if there were any nuclear weapons in Cuba, or that it believed there

117. Telegram no. 1194, State to USUN, November 5, 1962, p. 1 (Top Secret; now declassified).

118. Telegram no. 1223, State to USUN, November 7, 1962, p. 2 (Top Secret; now declassified).

119. Telegram no. 1856, USUN to State, November 19, 1962, p. 8.

probably were not. On the other hand, it could not seek to inspect the removal of something it did not believe was there. It did not wish to acknowledge the probable absence, or even doubt as to the presence, of nuclear warheads and possibly stimulate any Soviet temptation to conceal and keep in Cuba any warheads it might have there. In real terms, the Soviet leaders would almost certainly have been every bit as interested as the American leaders in promptly returning to the Soviet Union any nuclear warheads sent to Cuba. But worst-case military calculations, and domestic political realities, would not permit an explicit American judgment to that effect.

The result was agreement that "any [nuclear] warheads" for the missiles and bombs for the bombers were being returned. American surveillance and intelligence did not detect the return of any nuclear warheads to the Soviet Union, tending (except for the most suspicious) to confirm the estimate that none had been there.[120] Most significant, in the subsequent quarter of a century there have been no indications that any nuclear weapons were in Cuba.

The negotiations with respect to submarine basing—years later to become very important—tended to be "lost" in the concentration on the IL-28s. When on November 2 Stevenson had sent Mikoyan the list of offensive weapons, it included naval missiles in a category together with medium-range land-based missiles: "surface-to-surface missiles including those designed for use at sea."[121] By the time of the scaled-back instructions with the

120. One ship, the *Aleksandrovsk*, departed Cuba on November 5 and on November 23 unloaded in the Soviet Union six probable missile nose-cone *vans*, used for carrying warheads from storage facilities to the launch pads (where they would be married to the missiles). But this was not an indication that the actual nose-cones with warheads had ever arrived in Cuba. On November 9 a U.S. helicopter registered an uncertain "possible" detection of radioactivity from the freighter *Bratsk* leaving Cuba, but a more sensitive check two days later found no radioactive emanations from the ship.

121. Letter, Stevenson to Mikoyan, November 2, 1962. While ambiguous, the negotiating history makes clear that the short-range missiles on naval patrol craft in Cuba were not raised by the United States, and the logical assumption was that the broad language was intended to cover submarine-launched missiles. The "forgotten" list was not, however, really discussed or clarified with the

November 8 list, and throughout in the actual discussions, sea-based missiles (never in Cuba, except for the short-range missiles on patrol boats) were forgotten.

On November 3 President Kennedy clarified his instructions in a message to Stevenson and McCloy. Again, the main thrust was to reaffirm the importance of removing the IL-28s, but the president also sought to clarify "our policy and purpose": "In blunt summary, we want no offensive weapons and no Soviet military base in Cuba, and that is how we understand the agreements of October 27 and October 28." Moreover, the instruction noted that "there is some evidence of an intent to establish a submarine-tending facility" and was explicit on the *American* position with respect to a submarine base: "All the offensive weapon systems, including anything related to a submarine base, must be removed, or we shall have to consider further action of our own to remove them."[122] Following this strong and explicit statement of the American position, the very next day (November 4) McCloy raised the matter with Kuznetsov, and also said more generally that we would object to establishment of a Soviet military base in Cuba. Kuznetsov denied that the Soviet Union was building a submarine base, referring to Khrushchev's assurances to Ambassador Kohler concerning Mariel on October 16. On the general subject of objecting to bases, he said he understood that point of view—and how about U.S. bases in Turkey?

Following receipt of the report on the McCloy conversation with Kuznetsov, the Ex Comm in its next meeting on November 5 considered this exchange unsatisfactory and again instructed the negotiators in New York to tie down a commitment against construction of a submarine base. The fishing port at Mariel was no longer of concern, but the Ex Comm did want to obtain a Soviet commitment as to the future. The matter was not, however, raised in the next meeting of the negotiators in New York on November 6. Another instruction was then sent on November 7, but the matter

---

Soviet negotiators; discussion concentrated almost exclusively on the IL-28 bombers.

122. Telegram no. 1189, pp. 1, 2, and 4.
The "evidence" on the submarine-basing facility did not prove to be valid.

was not again addressed in the New York negotiations, which remained focused on the removal of the IL-28 bombers and on the issue of verification arrangements in Cuba. The president did, however, raise the matter in a letter to Khrushchev on November 6. He stated, "I hope you will understand that we must attach the greatest importance to the personal assurances you have given that submarine bases will not be established in Cuba."[123] Khrushchev did not comment further on this subject.

Ultimately, the Ex Comm in its twenty-eighth meeting on November 20 approved a settlement of the issues and lifting of the quarantine, *without* further consideration of the question of submarine bases. The resolution of the existing problems had simply taken precedence over potential longer-term issues.

Beginning as early as President Kennedy's letter of November 6, but most pointedly in a statement by McCloy to Kuznetsov on November 18, the United States also raised the matter of withdrawal of the four reinforced regiments, or "combat teams," the existence and extent of which had been belatedly discovered by American surveillance during the first half of November.[124] But the United States did not insist on more than the Soviet assurance that military personnel associated with offensive systems, including their protection, would be withdrawn. President Kennedy did pursue the matter privately with Khrushchev in early 1963, and in early February Khrushchev agreed to withdraw several thousand more Soviet military personnel from Cuba. Secretary Rusk repeatedly stated publicly in the first half of 1963 that the continued presence of Soviet troops in Cuba was "not acceptable" to the United States.[125] But there was no Soviet commitment to withdraw

123. Letter, Kennedy to Khrushchev, November 6, 1962.

Even drafts of President Kennedy's letter of November 6, 1962, have now been declassified, although to my knowledge never discussed in print. From the drafts, it is now known that the language on submarine basing replaced the following more categorical draft statement on the subject: "We would be bound to regard any move to establish a submarine base in Cuba just as seriously as we regarded the installation of missile bases and bombers."

124. Telegram no. 1856, pp. 5–6. See footnote 30 above for further discussion of these forces.

125. Rusk either raised the subject of Soviet troops in Cuba, or responded to

all Soviet military personnel. The four regimental combat teams were withdrawn, but some of the troops may have remained in a combination guard and training unit, as well as the air defense units manning the SAM antiaircraft missile sites, and other training specialists. The continuing Soviet military presence was a source of agitation to some American politicians for months thereafter, but did not become a major public issue.[126]

One incident, never before disclosed, that occurred in the midst of these negotiations from October 28 to November 20 may have affected the American position favorably, but it was not planned by or even known to the Ex Comm. By November 8 the United States had begun perceptibly to stiffen its insistence on the IL-28s and other issues at dispute, including what the Soviets could only see as an effort to backpedal on what was, for them, the key question remaining: American assurances not to attack Cuba. On that date, a Cuban covert action sabotage team dispatched from the United States successfully blew up a Cuban industrial facility.[127] To the Soviets, this was probably seen as a subtle American reminder of its ability to harass and attempt to subvert the Castro regime.

In fact, on October 30, after the peak of the crisis, the United States had belatedly suspended its Mongoose covert operations in

questions of news correspondents, on January 27, February 1, 13, 26, March 12, April 18, 28, and May 29, 1963. See *State Bulletin,* vol. 48 (January–June 1963), pp. 238, 245, 313, 388, 470, 686, 733, 934. While he said the presence of Soviet troops in Cuba was not "normal" or "acceptable," it was accepted.

126. On September 23, 1963, the Senate voted on an amendment proposed by Senator Goldwater to the Limited Nuclear Test Ban Treaty that would have postponed implementation of the treaty provisions until all Soviet troops had been removed from Cuba. The amendment was defeated by a vote of 75 to 17. That, in effect, ended the issue until its rebirth in 1979.

At the time of the 1979 "mini-crisis" over the Soviet brigade in Cuba, McGeorge Bundy wrote an article accepting responsibility for letting the issue fade away in 1963–64. See McGeorge Bundy, "The Brigade's My Fault," *New York Times,* October 23, 1979.

127. On November 13 the Cubans publicly claimed they had smashed a CIA sabotage team, but did not publicize the actual action five days earlier.

Another of the teams had been prevented on October 25 from destroying facilities at the Matahambre copper mine. I do not know if that was publicly disclosed by the Cuban authorities.

Cuba—once it had accidentally been learned that they were still going on! At the end of October, a new mission was about to be dispatched by Task Force W operating out of Miami. One of the operatives was sufficiently uneasy about such an operation just after the great Kennedy-Khrushchev agreement to end the crisis that he got a message to Robert Kennedy to verify that the mission was in order. As noted, the Mongoose infiltration and sabotage operations had been reinvigorated earlier in the month. But the operation had been forgotten when the crisis was resolved. The new mission was hastily called off, and all infiltration and attack operations against Cuban soil suspended. General Edward Lansdale was sent to Miami to ensure that operations were closed down. But three of ten six-man sabotage teams planned earlier in October to be sent into Cuba had already been dispatched and were beyond recall. One of them, on November 8, carried out its mission.[128]

While this incident was never raised in the U.S.-Soviet talks, and was unknown to most if not all members of the Ex Comm, it may have reinforced Soviet interest in a settlement. It surely must have reinforced Castro's doubts that the United States had really agreed to anything.[129]

The final item on the agenda, so far as American interests were concerned, was the commitment in Khrushchev's letter of October 28 to inspection under UN auspices in Cuba to verify the removal of the offensive arms. This issue remained stalemated. The removal of the missiles, and later the bombers, was satisfactorily arranged,

128. For this account of the October 30 standdown of operations, see Schlesinger, *Robert Kennedy*, pp. 533–34; and Prados, *Presidents' Secret Wars*, p. 214; and see *Alleged Assassination Plots*, pp. 147–48. The November 8 incident has not been reported in any previous publication.

129. On November 15, in a letter to the UN secretary general, Castro referred directly to this incident as buttressing his objection to the continued U.S. reconnaissance overflights. He stated: "The capture of the leader of a group of spies trained by the CIA and directed by it, here in Cuba, has shown us how the photographs taken by spying planes serve for guidance in sabotage and in their operations and has also revealed, amongst other things, a desire to cause chaos by provoking the deaths of 400 workers in one of our industries." The letter was passed to the United States by the United Nations, in unofficial UN translation, and was cabled to Washington in telegram no. 1802, USUN to State, November 15, 1962, p. 3 (Secret; now declassified).

with Soviet assistance. The United States had no real doubt that the offensive weapons had been removed. But it tied the question of verification against reintroduction of offensive arms to the question of American assurances against invasion.[130]

Castro, in addition to refusing to permit any foreign inspections on Cuban soil to verify the dismantling and removal, did offer his own terms for on-site inspection and verification. On November 25 he offered to allow inspection in Cuba, but only if there were also inspection of the dismantling of emigré Cuban "training camps for mercenaries, spies, saboteurs and terrorists; of the centers where subversion is prepared; and the bases from which pirate vessels set out for our coasts" in the United States and in Puerto Rico.[131]

All the matters I have been discussing here in the negotiations from October 28 to November 20—the IL-28s, nuclear weapons, submarine bases, army combat teams, and verification arrangements—have concerned American interests. The other major issue discussed throughout this period was the Soviet endeavor to obtain as formal, binding, and far-reaching an American commitment on noninvasion of Cuba as possible. Without reviewing the long series of exchanges on that subject, one can move to its conclusion. With the absence of agreement on verification in Cuba, the United States considered there was no basis to give more of a commitment than already implied by the exchange of letters on October 27–28.

President Kennedy's press conference statement of November 20 clearly spelled out the American position: "*If* all offensive weapons systems are removed from Cuba and kept out of the

130. President Kennedy, in his letter of October 27, had called upon the Soviet government to remove the offensive weapons in Cuba and to "undertake, with suitable safeguards, to halt the further introduction of such weapons systems into Cuba." In his reply of October 28 accepting this general deal, Khrushchev wrote only of dismantling and removing the weapons there and said, "We are prepared to come to an agreement with you to enable representatives of the UN to verify the dismantling of these systems." He said nothing about safeguards against future reintroduction of such systems.

131. Letter, Osvaldo Dorticós and Fidel Castro to U Thant, UN Security Council Document S/5280, November 26, 1962, pp. 1–6; reprinted in Larson, ed., "*Cuban Crisis*" *of 1962*, 2d ed., pp. 214–19; quotation on p. 218.

hemisphere in the future, under adequate verification and safeguards . . . we shall neither initiate nor permit aggression in this
hemisphere." In this same statement the president made clear that
while it had been promised that the IL-28s would be withdrawn,
and the missile sites had been dismantled and the missiles withdrawn under our surveillance, "important parts of the understanding of October 27 and 28 remain to be carried out. The Cuban
Government has not yet permitted the United Nations to verify
whether all offensive weapons have been removed, and no lasting
safeguards have yet been established against the future introduction
of offensive weapons back into Cuba."[132]

These conditions were not met.

The Soviets had been pressing for an American commitment
ever since the exchange of messages on October 28. Two days later
Gromyko had received Ambassador Kohler and sought to "codify"
the undertakings of both sides. Draft statements of assurances,
including a Soviet-Cuban draft formal protocol that looked like a
treaty, were all discussed in numerous meetings in New York, and
in at least six of the ten or more exchanges of letters between
President Kennedy and Khrushchev in November and December.

The most authoritative exchange on future commitments in the
negotiations resolving the 1962 crisis occurred in a meeting of First
Deputy Prime Minister Mikoyan with President Kennedy on November 29, 1962. Mikoyan repeatedly pressed for clarification and
confirmation that the U.S. accepted a commitment not to invade
Cuba. President Kennedy reassured him that the United States
had no intention of invading Cuba, but stressed that the conditions
called for in the exchange of letters in late October (international
verification in Cuba and safeguards) had not been met. Without
making the unequivocal future commitment the Soviets wanted,
Kennedy did state that if the Soviet Union abided by the exchange
of correspondence, so would the United States.[133]

132. "The President's News Conference of November 20, 1962," *Public
Papers: Kennedy, 1962*, p. 831.

133. No official American or Soviet account of this exchange has to date been
published. This brief account is based on the author's familiarity with the U.S.
record.

On January 7, 1963, Stevenson for the United States and Kuznetsov for the Soviet Union sent a joint letter to UN Secretary General U Thant stating that "while it has not been possible for our Governments to resolve all the problems that have arisen in connection with this affair, they believe that, in view of the degree of understanding reached between them on the settlement of the crisis and the extent of progress in the implementation of this understanding, it is not necessary for this item to occupy further the attention of the Security Council at this time."[134] The United States had made no pledge against invasion, and in the absence of verification measures in Cuba it continued its unilateral air reconnaissance. The Soviets made one final attempt to get American assurances when, on January 15, Soviet special envoy Kuznetsov also had a meeting with the president before he departed for Moscow. He, too, tried unsuccessfully to obtain a more binding U.S. commitment.

Seeking to put the best gloss possible on the outcome of the crisis, Khrushchev (on December 12 and on other occasions) and other Soviet spokesmen later publicly claimed that there was an American "pledge" not to invade—a claim not supported by any official American statement. As late as Khrushchev's speech to the Supreme Soviet on December 12, in which he laid down the official line on the whole crisis, he was evidently still expecting to be able to obtain a formal American commitment. He and his colleagues wished by that statement to put the whole matter behind them, but he could not avoid implicitly admitting that the American commitment was not all that they had sought. Thus on the one hand Khrushchev claimed: "The president declared quite definitely, and the whole world knows, that the United States would not attack Cuba and would also restrain its allies from such actions," thus permitting the Soviet Union to withdraw the missiles, since they had sent the missiles to prevent an attack. But Khrushchev was still seeking more of a commitment, so at a time when Americans, and the world, considered the crisis long settled,

134. Letter, Adlai Stevenson and Vasily Kuznetsov to U Thant, UN Security Council Document S/5227, January 7, 1963, p. 1; reprinted in Larson, ed., *"Cuban Crisis" of 1962,* 2d ed., p. 230.

Khrushchev was saying only that "at present favorable conditions have been created for liquidating the dangerous crisis that arose in the Caribbean. Now it is necessary to bring the negotiations to completion, to put on record the agreement reached as a result of the exchange of messages between the government of the Soviet Union and the U.S. government, and to seal this agreement with the authority of the United Nations."[135] Yet this was never done, and as noted, on January 7 the two governments closed the issue with their joint note to the secretary general removing the item from the UN Security Council agenda. Soviet commentaries never refer to this inconclusive outcome.

American commentaries, too, have tended to overlook the inconclusive tailing off of negotiations seeking "verification" in Cuba and American assurances. The general understanding has, quite reasonably, taken as an assumption of political realities that the United States did not intend to invade Cuba. Moreover, criticisms from the right that the Kennedy administration had "sold out" a right to invasion were dismissed without rebuttal that we had retained full rights. Nonetheless, the United States did not in 1962–63 formalize a commitment assuring against possible invasion of Cuba.

135. "The Present International Situation and the Foreign Policy of the Soviet Union, Report by Comrade N. S. Khrushchev at the Session of the U.S.S.R. Supreme Soviet, December 12, 1962," *Pravda*, December 13, 1962, and in Pope, *Soviet Views on the Cuban Missile Crisis*, pp. 71–107.

The Aftermath

THE CUBAN missile crisis has had important long-term effects. Even during the crisis itself, some of us in the U.S. government, and I presume in the Soviet government as well, were thinking ahead to the aftermath. For example, I had argued for a tough stand on the removal of the missiles and the bombers, but also for movement toward a reduction in tensions after resolution of the crisis. In the memoranda of October 25 and 27, I suggested that the United States should, "while solving the Cuban base question with determination, forcefully reaffirm its readiness to reach agreements on arms control and disarmament" and other broader diplomatic arrangements.[136] Those doves who argued most strongly for seeking to resolve the crisis through diplomatic means sought not only to find matching concessions, but also to use the occasion to advance a more far-reaching political agenda. Most hawks, to the contrary, opposed any move toward a détente. There were, however, also those, including myself, who favored a tough stand on the question of removal of the offensive weapons, but also hoped that in the aftermath there could be movement toward a détente in U.S.-Soviet relations. Thus in another memorandum to Alexis Johnson, on October 29, on the "Significance of the Soviet Backdown for Future U.S. Policy," while calling for strength, I also stated "it is vitally important that the U.S. take the initiative in offering to negotiate on major issues between East and West."[137]

President Kennedy included in his key letter of October 27, as

136. See Appendix documents B and C.
137. See Appendix document E.

an incentive to Khrushchev, a statement that once the crisis was settled, the effect on easing tensions would make possible broader negotiations. And in his reply to Khrushchev's letter of October 28 he reiterated his agreement with Khrushchev that increased attention should be given to disarmament. There had not, however, been any consideration in the Ex Comm or decision by the president on specific disarmament or other negotiating positions beyond the terms of settlement of the immediate crisis.

The main work on possible future negotiations with the Soviet Union was carried out by a group under the guidance of Walt W. Rostow, in which I participated. After the crisis had passed its peak, a paper on "Post-Cuba [Crisis] Negotiations with the USSR" was prepared and circulated to the Ex Comm on November 9.[138] It foreshadowed negotiations for a hot line, nuclear nonproliferation, curbing space weapons, and other arms control measures. Khrushchev on October 27 specifically called for renewed nuclear test ban negotiations and President Kennedy agreed in his letter of October 28 acknowledging Khrushchev's acceptance of the settlement offered. In the private exchanges between the two leaders in November and December, not published with the October crisis correspondence, as the more immediate issues of IL-28s and U.S. noninvasion assurances faded, the nuclear testing question became more central.[139]

While I do not know what parallel planning for arms control and

138. At this writing, to my knowledge this memorandum has not been declassified. In addition, I do not now recall and available declassified records do not show whether the memorandum was in fact discussed in the Ex Comm. In any case, it did enter into the train of policy thinking in the government.

139. On December 19 Khrushchev devoted an entire message to the president to the test ban issue and indicated that—on the basis of what Ambassador Arthur Dean had told Kuznetsov on October 30—the Soviet Union was prepared for a comprehensive test ban providing two or three on-site inspections. Unfortunately, there had been a misunderstanding as to the American position, as Kennedy indicated in his response on December 28. Expert talks were agreed on but soon foundered over this issue. It did, however, prove possible to negotiate a ban on nuclear weapons testing in the atmosphere, oceans, and outer space. The Limited Nuclear Test Ban Treaty was signed in Moscow on August 5, 1963.

The most complete and accurate account of these developments is in Glenn T. Seaborg, *Kennedy, Khrushchev, and the Test Ban* (Berkeley: University of California Press, 1981), pp. 178–262.

other negotiations may have been under way in the Soviet Union, there must have been some at an early date.

In the United States, there was almost universal approbation for President Kennedy's handling of the crisis, and renewed—although sobered—confidence within the administration.

President Kennedy's remarkable speech at American University on June 10, 1963, set a new tone in U.S. relations with the Soviet Union, and contributed to the emergence of a limited détente. It stemmed directly from a new awareness by Kennedy of the need for improving relations and a new recognition of the possibility of doing so. He reiterated his desire for improved relations in an address to the UN General Assembly on November 20, only two days before his untimely death. While affected by the death of the president and a transition in leadership, the new policy continued in effect another year until it fell victim to the intensified commitment to the war in Vietnam.

In the Soviet Union, Khrushchev to some extent benefited from an initial rallying of the leadership to show solidarity in the first months after the crisis, but in the longer run the outcome of the affair undoubtedly contributed to his fall from power two years later. Indeed, on a number of issues he was under attack within the leadership from late 1962 until the sudden incapacitating illness of his chief challenger, Frol Kozlov, in April 1963. Save for that fortuitous event, Khrushchev might well have been ousted earlier. Kennedy's preparedness to give Khrushchev a confidential unilateral assurance that the U.S. Jupiter missiles would be withdrawn from Turkey and Italy within months may well have made the settlement deal sufficiently satisfactory from the standpoint of conservative party leaders and the military leadership to have contributed to his ability to recoup his own political position. Some of the events set in train by the limited détente of 1963–64 in Soviet-U.S. relations probably helped him for a time, but the long-term negative impact of the missile crisis on his standing remained.

There was a perceptible, if not complete, turn in Soviet policy toward the West after the crisis. One cannot be sure to what extent the experience of the crisis was responsible for the shift, but it very likely tempered Soviet ambitions, curbing their inclination to press some challenges, as over Berlin. It is also likely that the crisis opened up a degree of greater belief in the possibility of mutual accommodation. Soviet pronouncements after the crisis will be examined in the last chapter in the context of the long-term influence of the crisis. They suggest a certain interest in moving beyond the cold war, and a belief that the experience of the missile crisis would lead in that direction. But many other factors were at play, including the impact on Soviet policy of shifts of influence within the Soviet leadership, and naturally the range of opportunities and challenges and Soviet calculations about them. Suffice it here to repeat the general conclusion that the experience of the crisis probably did contribute to a degree of shift in Soviet policy toward détente.

It is often contended in the West that the missile crisis led the Soviet Union to build up its military power. A remark by Kuznetsov to McCloy is frequently cited as evidence. Having had to accede to American demands and failing to get from the United States the kind of noninvasion commitment the Soviets had sought, Kuznetsov was painfully aware of the weak bargaining position of the Soviet Union, and of the humiliating defeat the Soviet Union had suffered. I am sure he meant it when he said to John J. McCloy, as the Soviet missiles were being withdrawn: "You Americans will never be able to do this to us again."[140] It is, however, attributing too much to that statement to conclude or assert—as many who cite it do assert—that he was signaling that the Soviet Union would as a consequence of their crisis defeat build up their military power in ways or to a degree they would not otherwise have done. In the first place, the Soviet Union did *not* enter on a "crash" program of accelerated buildup of their strategic military power. Moreover, while they did later build up to rough parity with the United States (some would say to more than parity), that was not due to the missile crisis. That buildup would have occurred in any case and was stimulated not only by the missile crisis in late 1962, but by the rapid Kennedy administration buildup set in motion in 1961.

The record clearly shows the turn toward détente and arms control. Within a year, three important arms control agreements

140. Charles E. Bohlen, *Witness to History, 1929–1960* (New York: W. W. Norton, 1973), pp. 495–96.

were reached: in June it was agreed to establish a hot line (in Soviet parlance, the "Red Line") direct communications link between Washington and Moscow; in August the Limited Nuclear Test Ban Treaty was signed; and in September U.S.-Soviet agreement was reached to support a UN General Assembly resolution banning the placing of nuclear weapons or other weapons of mass destruction into space (codified in 1967 in the space treaty).[141]

The experience of the missile crisis, in addition to stimulating these three agreements in 1963, also contributed to the resolve of both sides to agree on the Treaty on the Non-Proliferation of Nuclear Weapons (NPT), even though agreement was not reached until 1969. Similarly, it contributed to efforts to reach agreement on strategic arms limitations, although it was not until 1969 that the SALT negotiations began and not until 1972 that the first arms limitation agreements were reached.[142]

Also, there was no new Berlin crisis. While the precise relationship of this fact to the October 1962 crisis can only be conjectured, I believe the absence of a new flare-up over Berlin in 1963 to be an important consequence of the outcome of the Cuban crisis. Indeed, there was no Berlin crisis in the years following, and in 1971 the Quadripartite Berlin Agreement effectively defused that long-standing point of contention.

Within NATO, there was relief over the resolution of the crisis and satisfaction with its favorable outcome. The only indirect specific consequence was the prompt decision to remove the Jupiters from Turkey and Italy and to replace them with a commitment to the alliance of ten American Polaris submarines. In the discussion, however, the idea of a multilaterally manned naval

141. The agreements on the hot line and the Limited Test Ban Treaty are widely known. The 1963 agreement on banning weapons in space is not. The Soviet Union was prepared in 1963 to conclude a treaty banning nuclear weapons in space; President Kennedy decided not to do so that soon after the controversial test ban treaty, but this was not publicly known. The fullest account is available in my article "Banning the Bomb in Outer Space," *International Security,* vol. 5 (Winter 1980–81), pp. 25–40.

142. Efforts undertaken from 1964 to 1968 to launch strategic arms talks were hampered by the disparity in U.S. and Soviet strategic forces, and only with the advent of strategic parity was fruitful negotiation on a basis of equality possible.

nuclear missile force was introduced. The idea had earlier been suggested by Ambassador Thomas Finletter, the U.S. representative to NATO. In the very first memorandum on planning for the removal of the Jupiters from Turkey, on October 30, Walt Rostow raised the possibility.[143] Such a force, later termed the Multilateral Force (MLF), was discussed from 1963 to 1966 but never created.

Nor was there any renewed threat of an American invasion of Cuba. The United States did, however, continue to conduct an active policy of seeking to undermine and displace the Castro regime, including continued covert operations against Cuba.

In the aftermath of the crisis, American policy toward Cuba badly needed redefinition. Policy papers began to be written even before the crisis ended, and on December 4 the Ex Comm discussed "Future Policy toward Cuba."

One step was taken in the conclusion of semiofficial exchanges that had begun months earlier to arrange release of the survivors of the Bay of Pigs. On December 22, 1962, the 1,113 prisoners, veterans of the ill-fated "Brigade 2506" (and twenty Cuban CIA agents also captured), were freed and turned over to the United States in exchange for nearly $54 million worth of medical supplies and baby food. The arrangement was negotiated by James B. Donovan, who had also arranged the swap of spies that obtained the release of Francis Gary Powers, the U-2 pilot shot down over Sverdlovsk on May Day 1960. In a bizarre twist the CIA decided to use this opportunity to send as a gift from Donovan to Castro, an avid scuba diver, a diving outfit impregnated with bacteriological agents. Donovan, for whatever reason, discarded it and bought another diving suit to give Castro.[144]

The veterans of the Bay of Pigs brigade were personally welcomed by President Kennedy on December 29, against the advice of both Dean Rusk and McGeorge Bundy; it was essentially a domestic political and personal decision. Kennedy extemporane-

143. See memorandum for Mr. [McGeorge] Bundy from W. W. Rostow, "Turkish IRBM's," October 30, 1962, p. 2 (Secret; now declassified).

144. Prados, *Presidents' Secret Wars*, p. 215; and Schlesinger, *Robert Kennedy*, pp. 534–37; Larson, ed., *"Cuban Crisis" of 1962*, 2d ed., p. 358. Donovan had seen Castro as late as October 20, just before the crisis broke.

ously injected in his speech to them a promise to see their brigade flag in "a free Havana."[145] The brigade veterans then went on to other things.[146]

Covert action program Mongoose, as noted earlier, had been suspended on October 30. The future of Mongoose was on the Ex Comm agenda for the thirty-first meeting on November 29, but it is not clear if it was discussed then. There was also a problem of what to do with *another* Cuban brigade, trained in 1961–62, not committed at the Bay of Pigs. On January 25, 1963, the Ex Comm considered what to do with this other brigade and with Mongoose.[147]

In January–February 1963 the Ex Comm and the Special Group (Augmented) were replaced by a "Standing Group" of the NSC; Mongoose was abolished; the CIA Task Force W was merged into its Miami station (which remained, with Desmond FitzGerald replacing William K. Harvey).[148]

On November 29 at the Ex Comm meeting President Kennedy requested the State Department to develop a long-range plan to "keep pressure on Castro." Yet as early as January 4, 1963, McGeorge Bundy proposed exploring the possibility of communicating with Castro.[149] The Ex Comm, later the Standing Group, at their January 25 meeting, and others subsequently, developed a plan for several somewhat disparate paths of action to meet

145. Schlesinger, *Robert Kennedy*, p. 538.

146. Many entered a new special military training program set up by the United States that lasted until late 1965, involving in all some 2,700 men. Sixty-one of these, mostly Brigade 2506 veterans, were eventually granted American citizenship and entered the U.S. Army. (One, originally a military cadet under Batista, was by the mid-1980s a full colonel and the U.S. Army action officer for Central American and Caribbean affairs, actively boosting the Contras and still eager to see Castro overthrown.) Others entered the CIA, some being sent to the Congo in 1964 (the first introduction of armed Cubans into African civil wars), others breaking into Watergate in 1972, and still others mining ports in Nicaragua in 1984.

147. See Prados, *Presidents' Secret Wars*, p. 215; and Coordinator of Cuban Affairs, "Memorandum for the National Security Council's Executive Committee—United States Policy toward Cuba," January 25, 1963, pp. 1–8 (Confidential; declassified with considerable deletion).

148. See *Alleged Assassination Plots*, p. 170.

149. See Schlesinger, *Robert Kennedy*, p. 538.

divergent aims. The United States wanted to see Castro removed, but if that were not to be, then it wanted him to be as independent of the Soviet Union as possible. Policy papers therefore posed as objectives both "encouraging and supporting any developments within Cuba that offer the possibility of *divorcing* the Cuban Government from its support of Sino-Soviet Communist purposes," and simultaneously "encouraging and supporting any developments within Cuba that offer the possibility of *replacing* the Cuban Government with a regime that would break with the Sino-Soviet Bloc, it being understood that our ultimate objective is replacement of the regime by one fully compatible with the goals of the United States."[150] These objectives, in practice, were contradictory and clashed. Even to attempt to divorce Cuba from the Soviet Union would require contacts and incentives, which ran against the idea of replacing Castro's rule.

And American policy, in practice, was contradictory. In March and April 1963 covert sabotage operations were discontinued, and attempts were made to crack down on similar unauthorized Cuban emigré operations by such groups as Alpha 66. But on June 19, a new sabotage program was launched. Similarly, while covert CIA assassination attempts against Castro (not discussed in the Standing Group, the 303 Committee, which controlled covert activities, or any other interagency body) through the Mafia were abandoned, a new channel was opened. This renewed assassination attempt, through former Castro comrade-in-arms Rolando Cubeles Secades (who had been recruited by the CIA in 1961), led to a tragic irony. On November 22, 1963, the day that President John F. Kennedy was assassinated, Desmond FitzGerald in Paris supplied Cubeles with a poison pen to give Castro. Covert American-directed operations, raids, and assassination plots did not end until 1965.[151]

At the same time, steps were taken through two authorized

150. Coordinator of Cuban Affairs, "Memorandum . . . United States Policy toward Cuba," p. 2; emphasis in original. Note that an initial successor "regime" could be of any stripe; ultimately the United States wanted a government in Cuba compatible with both our democratic ideals and our own national interest.

151. See *Alleged Assassination Plots,* pp. 170–75; Schlesinger, *Robert Kennedy,* pp. 533–49; and Prados, *Presidents' Secret Wars,* p. 216.

semiofficial channels from September to December 1963 to develop a contact with Castro and sound out ways of ameliorating relations.[152]

The aftermath of the missile crisis, in sum, left American policy toward Cuba hostile, but with some beginnings of a belief that the United States should accept the Castro communist regime as a fact of life.

Soviet relations with Cuba were also left in need of redefinition in the aftermath of the crisis. Castro's anger and disenchantment remained, but so did his dependence on the Soviet Union—if anything, it was greater than before. The equivocal American "promise" not to invade was not taken as a real assurance.

In April–May 1963 Castro visited Moscow, for the first time and for more than a month. He and the Soviet leaders worked out a modus vivendi, despite continuing differences. At the close of the visit, Castro overcame his resentment enough to pay a glowing tribute to his hosts and benefactors. After recalling that in World War II the Soviet Union had lost more lives than the entire population of Cuba, he praised the Soviet Union because it "did not hesitate to assume the risks of a severe war in defense of our little country. History has never known such an example of solidarity. *That* is internationalism! *That* is communism!"[153]

During the mid-1960s, Cuban and Soviet foreign policy nonetheless continued to diverge in a number of respects. Cuba sought to develop a more independent line in the nonaligned world, one that placed a greater stress than did the Soviets on revolutionary action. While in some respects his inclinations coincided with Chinese criticisms of the Soviet Union, Castro in no way became a "Maoist." Rather, he sought to champion a genuinely third world Cuban communism, though with little success.

The divergence with Soviet policy reached a climax in 1968, when Castro toyed with echoing Eurocommunist criticism of the Soviet-led invasion of Czechoslovakia. The Soviets privately let

152. See Schlesinger, *Robert Kennedy,* pp. 551–58; and *Alleged Assassination Plots,* pp. 173–74.

153. "Speech by Prime Minister Fidel Castro of Cuba," *Pravda,* May 24, 1963.

Castro know in no uncertain terms that they would cut off all economic assistance if such criticism persisted. He capitulated. Thereafter Cuban foreign policy increasingly came into line with Soviet policy.

If there was an opportunity for the United States in the years 1963–68 to develop a relationship that could have weaned Castro away from the Soviet Union, it was missed. One cannot be certain that there was a real possibility, but one also cannot be certain that there was not at least the chance for a partial change in Cuban alignment.

STAGE 6

The Afterlife

THE MISSILE crisis not only had an aftermath in its effects on subsequent U.S.-Soviet relations (and Soviet-Cuban relations, and indirectly other developments not reviewed here), but also had a series of resurrected aftershocks or an "afterlife."

In the years following the missile crisis it became abundantly clear that the Soviet Union was not disposed to attempt again to deploy elements of its strategic nuclear power in Cuba, and that the United States was not disposed to invade or support an invasion of Cuba. In that fundamental respect the settlement was solid. It was not, however, until 1970 that it became clear that there *was* a 1962 Soviet-American "understanding" of continuing, or newly activated, validity. The United States had never issued any public or official statement of a commitment not to invade Cuba after the highly conditional statement by President Kennedy of November 20, 1962—the conditions of which (an international inspection in Cuba to verify the continuing absence of offensive arms) had not been met. This studied silence on a U.S. commitment was a considered position maintained throughout the Kennedy and Johnson administrations.[154]

The matter was unexpectedly raised for clarification by the Soviet side in August 1970—shortly *before* the United States became aware of the start of construction of a Soviet submarine

154. As the action officer in the Department of State on such matters during most of the 1960s, I drafted or cleared several later letters replying to congressional inquiries, provided press guidance, and in other ways ensured that the United States government did *not* state that it had accepted a formal noninvasion commitment.

94

base at Cienfuegos in Cuba. Chargé Yuli M. Vorontsov met with National Security Adviser Henry Kissinger on August 4, 1970, seeking assurances of American acceptance of the "understanding" of 1962. After reviewing the 1962 record, Kissinger became aware and advised the president that an understanding was, as he put it, "never formally buttoned down" in 1962: "It emerged that there was no formal understanding in the sense of an agreement, either oral or in writing." Nixon and Kissinger nonetheless decided, without consulting others (including the secretaries of state and defense), that it would be useful to tie Moscow down by taking the opportunity the Soviets had unaccountably proffered to "reaffirm" and activate the spongy 1962 understanding. So Kissinger assured Vorontsov on August 7 that the United States regarded the understanding as in effect, and "noted with satisfaction" that the Soviet Union also regarded it as "still in full force."[155]

The reason for the Soviet initiative in raising the 1962 Cuban understanding in August 1970 was unclear and perplexing. Kissinger, writing years later in his memoir, still found it "hard to imagine" why the Soviets had raised the matter in view of their own actions then under way to test and weaken the constraint. One possibility was that the Soviet leaders sought to reassure the United States that the submarine base they were preparing to build was not a step toward the placing of land-based missiles again in Cuba, in the hope that the United States would then acquiesce to the submarine base.

Kissinger had, as it turned out, jumped to a conclusion with respect to Vorontsov's message. "What he had come to convey," states Kissinger, "was his government's desire to reaffirm the Kennedy-Khrushchev understanding of 1962 with respect to Cuba." This way of putting the matter suggests unaccountable Soviet interest to reaffirm their acceptance of the constraints imposed. Fortunately, Kissinger accompanies his own interpretation with a

155. See Henry A. Kissinger, *White House Years* (Boston: Little, Brown, 1979), pp. 632–35. The first time that even key officials in the U.S. government who were involved in the Cienfuegos incident a month later learned of this prior August exchange of assurances was this revelation by Kissinger in his memoir nine years later.

verbatim quotation from Vorontsov's démarche: "We would like
to stress that in the Cuban question we proceed as before from the
understanding on this question reached in the past and we expect
that the American side will also strictly adhere to this understanding."[156] It is clear from this statement that the Soviet purpose was
to elicit an *American* reaffirmation of the understanding, rather
than to stress their own desire to reaffirm it, although of course
their reaffirmation was also entailed.

A senior Soviet official directly involved in the matter at the
time informed me some years later that the Soviet Union had raised
the matter because of Cuban concern over a possible American
attack. While Soviet intelligence did not confirm that possibility,
he said, Moscow still concluded it should elicit American reaffirmation of the understanding. It could then reassure Castro that it
had taken the matter up with the Americans and that there would
be no American intervention. The Soviets had a strong incentive
to avoid precipitating a new crisis centered on Cuba. Only two
years earlier Castro had agreed to return to the Soviet fold, and
then because of Soviet economic pressures, and the Soviets did
not wish again to arouse Cuban fears at being endangered by the
budding Soviet rapprochement with the United States.

The 1962 understanding was thus *consummated* only on August
7, 1970, when for the first time American leaders unequivocally
accepted continuing mutual commitments.[157] The Soviet commitment, in addition to being affirmed in the note delivered by
Vorontsov, was soon thereafter publicly reaffirmed in an "authorized" TASS statement on October 13, 1970, which declared that
the Soviet Union was not doing and would not do anything that

156. Ibid., p. 632.

157. The texts of the Soviet note of August 4 and the American reply of
August 7, 1970, have not been made public, but as stated in Kissinger's memoir
account the United States reiterated the understanding "as prohibiting the
emplacement of any offensive weapon of any kind or any offensive delivery
system on Cuban territory"—without redefining those terms carried over from
1962. Ibid., p. 634. President Nixon, more loosely, thought there was a 1962
understanding, and described the existing understanding as barring the Soviets
from putting *nuclear weapons* on Cuban territory; see Richard Nixon, *RN: The
Memoirs of Richard Nixon* (New York: Grosset and Dunlap, 1978), p. 486.

would "contradict the understanding reached between the Governments of the USSR and the United States in 1962."[158] And on November 13, 1970, there followed the first public American confirmation of an understanding, when a State Department spokesman awkwardly noted President Kennedy's statement of November 20, 1962, and the TASS statement of October 13, 1970, as the basis for a conclusion that "we are confident that there is an understanding by the two Governments of the respective positions on the limits of their actions with regard to Cuba."[159] Thus, the "understanding" projected in November of 1962 was not really consummated until August of 1970, and not confirmed publicly until October of that year. Both governments, however, preferred to gloss over the past uncertainties and differences and to attribute the understanding to their predecessors of 1962.

While the Soviet activation of the 1962 understanding in August 1970 was prompted by renewed Cuban concerns, it was followed almost immediately by a near-crisis precipitated by a Soviet action probing the edge of the constraints on its actions and the American reaction. There is no need to review the issue in detail, as it goes beyond the subject of this study and has been done elsewhere.[160] It is, however, useful to consider how it related to the Cuban missile crisis, not only in terms of defining the formal obligations of the 1962/1970 settlement, but more basically how it reflected the longer-term impact of the 1962 crisis.

In the late summer of 1970, as the leaders of the United States and the Soviet Union were moving tentatively toward what became the détente of the 1970s, a significant incident occurred. No sharp public clash or crisis arose, and the issue was resolved by quiet diplomacy. Nonetheless it was significant because of what it represented to the leaders on both sides with respect to conflict management in a new era of political relations and under an

158. TASS, in *Pravda,* and on Radio Moscow, October 13, 1970.

159. Robert McCloskey, Department of State press briefing, November 13, 1970. Note the unusual character of the statement, indicating the lack of previous "confidence" in the existence of such an understanding.

160. See my article "Handling the Cienfuegos Crisis," *International Security,* vol. 8 (Summer 1983), pp. 46–66.

emerging new strategic relationship. The Soviet leaders were seeking to test the relationship of the two powers in a dawning age of strategic, and they hoped political, parity. And the American leaders were seeking to contain what they regarded as Soviet expansionist impulses and to "manage" the emergence of Soviet power under the new conditions of parity.

The incident was precipitated by the Soviet construction of a submarine base in Cienfuegos Bay on the southern coast of Cuba, clearly with the intention of using this base to support its own expanding naval presence on the world ocean, if the United States were to acquiesce. One reason for the special significance of the probe was the unusual neuralgia over Cuba in the United States from the time Castro took power, especially after the resounding defeat for the United States at the Bay of Pigs in 1961, which was only partly offset by the American success in the Cuban missile crisis confrontation.[161] The other reason was the neuralgia of the Soviet leaders over the constraints imposed in the settlement of the Cuban missile crisis. Thus, apart from the intrinsic significance of Soviet submarine basing—providing certain measurable advantages to the Soviet Union and corresponding disadvantages for the United States—the establishment of a base for Soviet missile-carrying submarines would have marked a symbolic repeal of the American imposition of limits on Soviet freedom of action in 1962.

From the American perspective, the missile crisis had resulted from a surreptitious Soviet deployment of medium- and intermediate-range strategic missiles in Cuba, despite earlier clear public warning against such an action by the American president, and despite false denials and assurances from the Soviet leadership. The United States had successfully deterred a provocative Soviet deployment that would have altered the balance (that is, diluted the American preponderance) of strategic military power, and

---

161. President Nixon had a special sensitivity, and hostility, to Cuba, dating from the time of Castro's rise to power (on which John Kennedy had capitalized in narrowly defeating Nixon in the 1960 electoral campaign). One of Nixon's first acts in office in 1969 was to direct the CIA to intensify covert operations against Cuba—just as the CIA was winding down such actions through Miami-based exile groups. See Tad Szulc, *The Illusion of Peace: Foreign Policy in the Nixon Years* (New York: Viking, 1978), p. 175, although Szulc attributes the pressure to Kissinger, who in fact was acting at Nixon's insistent behest.

restored the political and military *status quo ante*. And we had reasserted the Monroe Doctrine and rebuffed a Soviet political as well as military encroachment on our vital interests in our own backyard, so to speak. The outcome was widely regarded as an outstanding American victory in the cold war.

From the Soviet standpoint, the Soviet Union in 1962 had been under no obligation to obey American unilateral injunctions against deploying weapons on the territory of an ally—precisely as the United States itself had done in a number of states immediately around the Soviet Union—nor to inform the Americans of their intention to do so. They were doing nothing illegal or improper under international law, nor indeed other than the United States itself had done. Then the United States had used its superior military power to compel their withdrawal of the missiles, humiliating them (despite such face-saving elements as an equivocal American promise not to invade Cuba and the informal secret statement of intention to withdraw American IRBMs from Turkey). The American action had been an offensive use of military power—compellence, not deterrence—and spurred Soviet resolve to acquire countervailing strategic military power. And while they would never admit it openly, they deeply nursed resentment that they had been compelled to give up a prerogative of great power status. The outcome of the Cuban missile crisis had been a rankling defeat in the cold war.

Hence in 1970, as the Soviet Union was acquiring strategic parity, the Soviet leaders sought to circumscribe the limitations imposed in 1962 on their military presence in Cuba, to erase that legacy from a time of American superiority and cold war, an imposed constraint not in keeping with "parity" with the United States as a global power, to which they now aspired.

The "mini-crisis" of 1970 arose in September and was resolved by October. Briefly, the facts were these: on September 16, a U-2 reconnaissance plane photographed construction of a naval facility at Cay Alcatraz in the Bay of Cienfuegos that suggested preparation of a submarine-servicing facility. On September 9 a Soviet flotilla including a submarine tanker, an ocean-going tug, and a ship carrying two special-purpose barges (recognized as a type used to support nuclear-powered submarines) had just arrived at

Cienfuegos. The U-2 mission had in fact been prompted both by the arrival of the flotilla, and by observation in an August flight of then-still-unidentified early construction.

President Nixon wanted to respond sharply but he also wanted to delay his response until after a scheduled European visit. The Pentagon favored a strong diplomatic action to evict the Soviets; the State Department favored more deliberate diplomatic clarification of the question. Kissinger did not want to delay, but the president decided to wait until after his trip. Then a press leak on September 25 (possibly inspired by Kissinger) led to a Pentagon press briefing on the details of the construction and the naval visit— a briefing made by mistake! Kissinger next entered the picture with a background briefing to the press by a "White House source" (all on that same day), recalling President Kennedy's statement of November 1962 in which he had outlined the understanding on nonstationing of Soviet offensive weapons in Cuba that resolved the Cuban missile crisis. Kissinger warned: "The Soviet Union can be under no doubt that we would view the establishment of a strategic base in the Caribbean with the utmost seriousness." That same day Dobrynin saw Kissinger, and was reported "ashen" (again!) from shock when Kissinger had spelled out the full basis for, and extent of, American concern.[162]

By early October the "crisis" was resolved. There would be no Soviet naval base in Cuba, and the understanding on nonstationing of offensive weapons was reaffirmed and made more explicit. On October 13 TASS publicly denied that the Soviet Union was building a submarine base in Cuba and confirmed that the Soviet Union would continue to adhere to the understanding. Moscow thus clearly accepted a Soviet commitment under the 1962 understanding not to establish a missile submarine base in Cuba. The Soviet attempt to reduce the constraints imposed in 1962 had not succeeded, but there had been no public confrontation and no public backing-down.

162. See Kissinger, *White House Years,* pp. 632–52. For background on the Cienfuegos episode, see also Garthoff, "Handling the Cienfuegos Crisis," *International Security,* pp. 46–66; and *Soviet Naval Activities in Cuba,* Hearings before the Subcommittee on Inter-American Affairs of the House Committee on Foreign Affairs, 91 Cong. 2 sess. (GPO, 1971).

The Soviet Union did not want to jeopardize what they had treated since 1962 as an American commitment not to act militarily against Cuba, even though the American side conspicuously had never confirmed such a commitment. Hence the successful Soviet effort in August to reinforce the overall 1962 "understanding," with its American commitment, before their probe of the American position on submarine basing. This history also explains why the American administration also wished to date the U.S. commitment to 1962, and to state that the 1970 understanding merely "reaffirmed," "clarified," and "amplified" the 1962 understanding to cover Soviet submarine missile systems. Overall, in 1970 the United States got a greater degree of Soviet commitment against permanent missile submarine basing in Cuba, while the Soviet Union finally got an American commitment to the 1962 understanding and the pledge not to invade Cuba.

In May 1972, on the eve of the first summit meeting between President Nixon and General Secretary Brezhnev, the Soviets again probed the limits of the 1962/1970 constraint by sending a diesel-powered nuclear ballistic missile Golf-II class submarine to visit Cuba (not, however, Cienfuegos). While Nixon and Kissinger did not raise this missile submarine visit during the summit, the Soviet leaders had received a powerful signal of American displeasure. As the Soviet flotilla left Bahia de Nipe on May 6 (where a U.S. surveillance patrol had remained throughout its six-day stay, just six—not twelve—miles off the harbor entrance), the submarine submerged immediately outside the harbor entrance. The U.S. surveillance ships, aided by P-3 patrol aircraft (based at Guantánamo Bay in Cuba), made sonar contact and forced the submarine to surface. Several times at night this was repeated, with the Soviets even firing flares to discourage the P-3 aircraft, and with high-speed maneuvers by the Soviet and American ships; the submarine was repeatedly forced to surface until the Soviet formation was well into the Atlantic.[163]

All this was undoubtedly known to the Soviet leaders in Moscow

163. This entire incident became known only when revealed in 1980 by the retired former commander of the U.S. surveillance patrol; see Captain Leslie K. Fenlon, Jr., USN (ret.), "The Umpteenth Cuban Confrontation," *U.S. Naval Institute Proceedings,* vol. 106 (July 1980), p. 44.

during the summit. But incredible as it may seem to those not familiar with the workings of government bureaucracies, from all available evidence (including interviews with a number of the American participants), it appears that this entire incident was not known to President Nixon, or to Dr. Kissinger, in orchestrating policy then or even long after the event![164]

The Soviet leaders also tested the 1962 and 1970 "understand-ings" in another way. Shortly before the Cienfuegos confrontation in 1970, but not involved with it, the Soviet Union had begun occasional flights of Tu-95 *Bear* turbo-prop reconnaissance aircraft from Murmansk to Cuba over the North Atlantic. Then, soon after the summit, in September 1972 a new pattern began. Operational reconnaissance flights from Havana, returning to Cuba, began to occur, unlike the earlier flights where reconnaissance was inciden-tal to transit from the USSR to Cuba and return flights. These flights all involved the naval reconnaissance version of the *Bear* (the *Bear D*), not the air force bomber version.[165] The case of the Soviet reconnaissance *Bears* never became an issue between the United States and the Soviet Union. Of course, the American *non*-reaction *was* a response to Moscow, and the appropriate one since there was no good basis for a challenge.[166]

164. For a more detailed account of this episode, see Garthoff, "Handling the Cienfuegos Crisis," *International Security,* pp. 58–60.

165. The two versions of the aircraft are visually distinguishable, the recon-naissance version having a large observation bubble and no bomb bay.

166. Secretary of Defense Melvin Laird wrote to Secretary of State William P. Rogers in September 1972, after the first such reconnaissance mission along the U.S. East Coast, urging an immediate protest, and again in January 1973, after the first letter was not acted upon. In fact, at the State Department action level we had found no basis for charging the Soviets with violating the under-standings of 1962 or 1970, so far as the latter were known, but could only note that the White House was the only party that knew the full content of the earlier exchanges. The State Department at a senior level was orally instructed by Dr. Kissinger to "sit" on the Defense requests, and nothing was ever done.

This account is based on my direct involvement as deputy director of the Bureau of Politico-Military Affairs of the Department of State, 1970–73.

Kissinger had, in fact, raised the matter of the *Bear* flights with Dobrynin in 1972, seeking to curb Soviet expansion of such flights or their extension to include bombers, without challenging the Soviet right to occasional reconnaissance flights. He did not, however, report this fact to the Department of State or the Department

A decade later, in 1983, the Soviets began also to send flights of two Tu-142 antisubmarine warfare (ASW) versions of the *Bear* (the *Bear F*). This was accepted. They have never sent the bomber or air-launched cruise missile versions of the *Bear* aircraft, which would undoubtedly be challenged as not compatible with the 1962 and 1970 understandings.

In 1978, a brief alarm arose over the Soviet transfer of MiG-23 fighter-bombers to Cuba. The administration was able, after monitoring closely the situation in Cuba and after consulting the Soviet leadership, to reassure the public that there was no evidence that a nuclear attack capability was being provided, and that the Soviet authorities had given assurances that no nuclear capability would be provided—and, moreover, that the 1962 understanding would continue to be adhered to. The matter soon faded as a public issue, but not before again raising the question of what the 1962 understanding covered—clearly strategic offensive ballistic missiles, ballistic missile submarine bases, and Soviet strategic bombers. But what about MiG-23 fighter-bombers?[167]

Crated MiG-23 fighter-bombers had begun to arrive in Cuba in late April 1978. The first public reference to their introduction into Cuba was on October 30, and the first real attention was drawn to them by a syndicated article by Rowland Evans and Robert Novak on November 15, 1978. That article referred to a secret memorandum on the subject sent by Secretary of Defense Harold Brown to President Jimmy Carter on October 23.[168] A considerable brouhaha

---

of Defense at the time, nor cite it as a reason for non-action in 1973. (Information from a member of Kissinger's NSC staff.)

167. Some who in 1978 most vigorously challenged the compatibility of MiG-23s in Cuba with the 1962 understanding did so for other reasons—chiefly in order to raise doubts both as to Soviet trustworthiness and intentions, and as to the strength and steadfastness of the Carter administration. In particular, some opponents of a SALT II agreement sought to use the issue to brand the Soviets as "hard" and the administration as "soft" on a security question, and thereby to discredit both. Others wondered whether the Soviets were probing or "testing" the mettle of the United States.

168. Rowland Evans and Robert Novak, "Cuba's Mig 23s," *Washington Post,* November 15, 1978; and see Fred Hoffman, AP release, October 30, 1978, for the first public reference. Ironically, the purpose of the memorandum from Secretary of Defense Brown was precisely to alert the president to the *political*

developed in the press over the next two weeks. At a press conference on November 30, President Carter stated that the Soviet government had provided assurances that no shipments of arms to Cuba had or would violate the terms of "the 1962 agreement," and that we had no evidence of nuclear weapons in Cuba.[169] While not silencing all critics, this quieted most concerns.[170] The matter was laid to rest by a State Department statement on January 17, 1979, concluding that the MiG-23s in Cuba did not constitute a violation of "the 1962 agreement," that they were not configured for nuclear weapons delivery, and that there were not any nuclear weapons in Cuba.[171] Again in 1982, when a second squadron of MiG- 23s was sent to Cuba, there was a flurry in the new administration, but no issue was made of the matter.

Based on the record of 1962, it is clear that the introduction of limited numbers of MiG-23 fighter-bombers into the Cuban air force beginning in 1978 was not inconsistent with or in violation of any understanding between the U.S. and Soviet governments, so long as these aircraft were not given a substantial offensive capability by being armed with nuclear weapons.

In 1979 another mini-crisis of even greater moment arose over the belated discovery of the presence of a Soviet "combat brigade" in Cuba, possibly the descendant of one of the four introduced in 1962.[172] A question was again initially raised by some as to whether that presence violated "the 1962 understanding"; it was soon

---

sensitivity of the new findings about the brigade—a danger activated by the leak about the memorandum itself in the sensationalistic Evans and Novak article.

169. "The President's News Conference of November 30, 1978," *Weekly Compilation of Presidential Documents*, vol. 14 (December 4, 1978), p. 2101.

170. By December 8, even Evans and Novak had shifted targets and reported that "concern over Soviet shipments of Mig 23 attack aircraft to Cuba now centers not on possible Soviet violations of the 1962 Kennedy agreement so much as on Moscow's future targets for its all-purpose economy-sized Cuban mercenary force." See Rowland Evans and Robert Novak, "Those Cuban Migs," *Washington Post*, December 8, 1978.

171. Department of State, "Questions and Answers," press release, January 17, 1979.

172. For a detailed review of that crisis, see Raymond L. Garthoff, *Détente and Confrontation: American-Soviet Relations from Nixon to Reagan* (Brookings, 1985), pp. 828–48.

generally acknowledged that it did not, although other concerns and objections remained. In 1962 the Soviets had informed us they would withdraw the military personnel associated with the missile systems, and they did—but they did not promise, nor as earlier noted did we consistently press them, to remove all Soviet military personnel and refrain from introducing others in the future.

Some American advocates of a more hard-line policy toward Cuba and the Soviet Union have, over the years, suggested that the 1962 understanding included a ban on Cuban support or assistance to communist revolutionaries in other countries. That was not a part of the 1962 exchanges or negotiations settling the missile crisis. It is true that President Kennedy, in stating American policy, asserted that Cuba, and the Soviet Union through Cuba, should not export revolution. In his statement on November 20 marking the close of the crisis, President Kennedy stated that "if all offensive weapons systems are removed from Cuba and kept out of the hemisphere in the future, under adequate verification and safeguards, and if Cuba is not used for the export of aggressive Communist purposes, there will be peace in the Caribbean."[173] But those who have interpreted this to mean that the understanding of 1962 included a ban on Cuban support for communist revolutions in other countries have failed to recognize that there was no such undertaking by Khrushchev (to say nothing of Castro).[174] Equally important, they have misconstrued the reason that the president added that reference. He was under no illusion that his statement would add any Soviet or Cuban commitment; his reason for stating it was to loosen the *American* commitment not to invade Cuba. If there were a serious change in Cuba's role, he did not want the statement of U.S. intention not to initiate or permit aggression against Cuba to free Cuban hands to initiate aggression against any of its neighbors. In addition, of course, the proviso on "adequate verification and safeguards" was, at least in part, in the Khrushchev message, and the failure to implement it (to be sure, owing to recalcitrance by Castro, not Khrushchev) meant that the whole

173. *Public Papers: Kennedy, 1962*, p. 831.

174. See, for example, Jeane Kirkpatrick, "Our Cuban Misadventures," *Washington Post*, April 21, 1986.

understanding was one that the United States could escape it if wished. The Soviet Union and Cuba never accepted any commitment on nonsupport to revolutions in other countries, and were not even asked to do so, as part of the settlement of the missile crisis in 1962.

The United States government, at least until the Reagan administration, has never claimed such a broad interpretation of the 1962 understanding. And in the confirmation of an understanding in 1970, this matter was not included.

The Reagan administration has never formally charged a violation of the 1962/1970 understanding with the Soviet Union, nor asserted formally its interpretation of that understanding. There has been no charge of a violation made to the Soviet Union, nor cause to do so. The penchant of President Ronald Reagan and members of his administration to state their personal feelings publicly has, however, beclouded the matter somewhat. For example, on September 14, 1983, he stated to a group of reporters that "as far as I'm concerned, that agreement has been abrogated many times by the Soviet Union and Cuba in the bringing in of what can only be considered offensive weapons, not defensive, there."[175] The White House press spokesman, Larry Speakes, later explained that the president was referring to violations of the "spirit of the agreement, . . . in the light of all the Soviet military equipment that's been shipped into Cuba over the years." He also said the United States did not intend to abrogate its commitment under the agreement.[176] Reagan has not referred to the matter further.[177]

175. Francis X. Clines, "President Accuses Soviet on '62 Pact," *New York Times*, September 15, 1983.

176. Ibid.

177. Some other members of the Reagan administration have also made casual and unwarranted charges of Soviet violation of the 1962 understanding by supplying arms to Cuba. Most notably, see the interview with CIA Director William J. Casey, "The Real Threat in El Salvador—and Beyond," *U.S. News and World Report*, vol. 92 (March 8, 1982), pp. 23–24.

The Long-Term Legacy

TWENTY-FIVE years have now passed since the Cuban missile crisis, and despite serious international frictions there has not been another incident like it. Nonetheless the risks from any direct confrontation, even if small in probability, are enormous in potential consequence.

The United States and the Soviet Union are great powers with global interests, and sometimes those interests clash. *Crisis management* is necessary if crises arise; but *crisis prevention* and *crisis avoidance* based on political restraint and accommodation of differences are much to be preferred. Arms control limitations and reductions are important in their own right and because they can favorably affect political relations. Prevention of nuclear war, and hence prevention of any war involving the United States and the Soviet Union, is of highest priority. Nonetheless, since political efforts to resolve disputes peacefully are not always successful, we must be prepared to deal with and "defuse" any crises that may, despite our best efforts, occur. This includes the need to "de-escalate" crises, and still more any armed hostilities that might break out. Studying the experience and learning the lessons of the 1962 missile crisis, and to the extent possible doing so together, can help both the United States and the Soviet Union to ensure not only that such a crisis never recurs, but also that a greater catastrophe never occurs.

In the United States, greatest attention has been given to crisis management and more broadly to conflict management. This tendency is true in general, and with respect to study of the Cuban missile crisis. In the Soviet Union, on the other hand, the general

107

inclination and most attention given to the Caribbean crisis of 1962 has been directed to developing political accommodation and crisis prevention, rather than crisis management. Curiously reversing the usual stereotypes, the Americans have been sober, pessimistic realists, assuming that, regrettably, crises will occur and must be safely managed, while the Soviets have appeared to be more optimistic, if not hopelessly idealistic, in arguing that crises can and must be prevented by political collaboration. Under the surface, however, the American "realism" may spring from an idealistic faith that with a will anything can be managed, and the apparent Soviet belief in political accommodation may shield a deep pessimism over the ability of the two sides reliably to manage a crisis. The Soviet concentration on seeking political regulation of differences so as to preclude crises may be generated more by that concern than by conviction that the task of political settlement will be easy or necessarily successful.

Both Kennedy and Khrushchev were highly aware of the dangers of uncontrolled occurrences and of the situation acquiring a momentum that might escape their control. As the record shows, those concerns were well founded. Many events were interpreted by the other side as planned and controlled actions when in fact they were neither. Actions were undertaken on what one might term "inertial guidance"—something moving by its own momentum but no longer controlled or even remembered. Only when a U-2 accidentally overflew Soviet territory at the height of the crisis did anyone recall there were still U-2s flying near the Soviet Union. The Soviet shooting down of another U-2 over Cuba the same day, October 27, may have been the result of an action taken under standing rules of engagement forgotten in the Kremlin. (After all these years we still do not know.) When a CIA-dispatched sabotage team blew up a Cuban plant on November 8 it was almost certainly seen in Moscow (and certainly in Havana) as an intended signal, yet it was the result of an inadequately monitored covert action program that had been stimulated at the start of the crisis in mid-October—but then forgotten about while the crisis was being resolved (and not thought of again until October 30, when it was too late to recall three teams already sent in).

As for actions by third parties, what if Colonel Penkovsky's farewell signal had been taken seriously? The United States might well have then undertaken some further action (such as Defcon 1) that Moscow could have construed as preparation for immediate hostilities. The president's speech on Cuba might then have been seen, in suspicious Moscow intelligence, military, and even political circles, as a feint to cover American mobilization for a first strike. Soviet military doctrine in 1962 called for *Soviet* preemption if there was positive indication that the United States was preparing imminently and irrevocably for a first strike. SAC doctrine also called for preemption if a Soviet attack was imminent. In both cases, to be sure, ultimate political decision was predicated. But was it absolutely assured? One need not predict the outcome to say that the risk and danger to both sides could have been extreme, and catastrophe not excluded.

Other deliberate and intended actions had unanticipated and uncontrolled dimensions. The Defcon 2 SAC alert was ordered, but the flourish of open communication was neither authorized by or even subsequently known to the American leaders. Nor was the American leadership aware that the Jupiter missiles in Turkey were being turned over to Turkish control on October 22, although there is good reason to believe the fact had registered with Khrushchev.

Certainly President Kennedy and his principal advisers, and by all indications Chairman Khrushchev and his colleagues in the Soviet leadership, sensed at first hand that no other objective can be of greater importance than avoiding nuclear war. That judgment, by those leaders at that time and by their successors, does not of course mean that other objectives will not be pursued simultaneously. What it does mean is that in critical situations with a high risk of leading to war, leaders will seek solutions that involve compromise of their various conflicting objectives and interests.

A readiness to seek a compromise resolution of a crisis is, alone, no assurance agreement will be reached, but such readiness on both sides is probably a necessary condition. The nature of the compromise will vary with the case, depending on such factors as the nature of the issues, the perceived stakes, the resolve of the parties, and their respective relevant power.

One reason for the Soviet miscalculation of the American reaction to the missile deployment in Cuba was an incorrect assessment of the American stakes—as they would be weighed by the American leadership. The planned delay in disclosing the missiles to the United States until after the U.S. congressional elections was expected by the Soviet leaders to take care of any domestic political problem that President Kennedy might have in accepting the modest deployment. Evidently they greatly underestimated the complex of political considerations that would enter into the American decision. The Soviets also undoubtedly misjudged the solidarity the other Latin American countries would show in support of the United States' position under the circumstances that their own secret action had created. They also misjudged the general world reaction.

The Soviets learned from the experience the disadvantages of bluffing and especially of deception and disinformation. They gained nothing—and lost a great deal—by their deception of the American leaders about the deployment.

The United States, for its part, did not deter the Soviet Union from making its decision to deploy their missiles in Cuba and embarking on deployment. Several Ex Comm members, in retrospect, and later American analysts of the crisis, have concluded that the United States should have given stronger and clearer warnings earlier. Above all, earlier. Yet it is not easy to see how the Soviet course of action could have been predicted. (One of the principal authors of the national intelligence estimates in 1962, overstating this point, later argued that the *estimates* had not been wrong—Khrushchev had!) Quite simply it is hard to predict an irrational, or unsound, or simply unique initiative by another party.

Direct communication between the leaders, and secrecy of that and other diplomatic intercourse, were at least valuable and may have been essential to the working out of a mutually acceptable resolution of the crisis. This was the virtually unanimous judgment of those actually engaged on both sides and of later analysts of the missile crisis.

In President Kennedy's later continuing confidential exchange of letters with Khrushchev, after the latter had referred to the value of other confidential channels as well, Kennedy assured him that he too valued these contacts. But he also used the occasion to say: "I have not concealed from you that it was a serious disappointment to me that dangerously misleading information should have come through these channels before the recent crisis," referring to the message through Georgi Bolshakov.[178]

The Kennedy-Khrushchev exchanges did not of course lead either side to change its policy positions, but they did help to identify a basis for a compromise. Normal diplomatic channels were, in fact, essentially set aside, or at least adapted (for example, Robert Kennedy became the chief interlocutor with Ambassador Dobrynin). The unorthodox Fomin-Scali channel did contribute to the president's belief that Khrushchev's October 26 message (which was less explicit than Fomin's) would provide an acceptable basis. Kennedy nonetheless later cautioned Khrushchev about new, unofficial (and especially press) intermediaries, and this caution was appropriate. It was a desperate makeshift move because the Soviet leaders had "burned" their established informal channel—Georgi Bolshakov to Robert Kennedy. Not only had it been unwise to engage in a direct deception of the president, it also made the channel no longer credible.

Khrushchev and his colleagues no doubt believed in October as they had in May that they were justified in placing the missiles in Cuba. They discovered that their earlier judgment that the Americans would, reluctantly, accept the deployment, and the related belief that they could install such weaponry in secret and announce a fait accompli in their own time and way, were wrong. They did then recognize that the initiative in precipitating the crisis, if not the responsibility and blame, resided in their decision on deploying

---

178. Letter, John F. Kennedy to Nikita S. Khrushchev, December 14, 1962, p. 2 (now declassified).

Kennedy also used this occasion to criticize Soviet use of the Fomin-Scali channel, presenting it as something presumably not authorized by Khrushchev, a caution he did not extend to Bolshakov's disinformation. He mentioned in particular the hazards of using a member of the American media owing to the fierce competition of the press, their unaccountability to the U.S. government for what they report, and their penchant for later publicizing what they may learn privately. Ibid.

the missiles. This acknowledgment contributed to their readiness to make the larger share of concessions in order to resolve the crisis. The initiative is a factor both sides weigh in evaluating the stakes and deciding on elements of a compromise. The responsibility for the precipitating move, in other words, is an element in the balance of resolve.

The element that looms largest in most peoples' minds, and in many analyses, is the relative power of the two sides. This is undoubtedly a bedrock factor, but it is not the only one and often not even the one that determines the resolution of the crisis.

The United States had both local conventional and global nuclear superiority in 1962. The ability to effect the quarantine, and to pose credible threats of air strike and invasion, could not be countered by the Soviet Union. It would, however, be unwise to draw conclusions from the outcome of the Cuban missile crisis based on simple correlation with the balance of military forces.

The most basic element in one sense was the strategic nuclear balance. While neither side ever contemplated a resort to nuclear weapons, the American superiority undoubtedly contributed to Soviet caution against matching the American local conventional superiority around Cuba by a countermove at a place of Soviet local superiority such as Berlin. Contrary to a widely expressed view, I believe the outcome today under strategic nuclear parity would be the same. The Soviet failure to attempt to repeal the constraints of the 1962/1970 understanding about Cuba in the 1980s, or to test a comparable move in Nicaragua, I believe, bears strong witness to that fact. The reasons why they do not seek to test the U.S.-imposed constraint in Nicaragua are probably mixed, but that only underlines the fact that many considerations other than the strategic balance are involved and indeed usually determining.

Deterrence of moves that may precipitate a crisis is directly related to the matters of initiative, stakes, resolve, and relative power. If the United States leadership had known that the Soviet leaders were contemplating a missile deployment in the spring of 1962, they might have been able to convince the Soviet leaders not to do it. In that circumstance, with respect to the Cuban case in 1962, a strong private warning might have been enough. But mere warnings and other indications of strong feeling about something are usually not enough to deter a diplomatic political-military move, even a hostile one, that does not present a clear and present danger. For example, an American warning to the Soviet Union not to intervene in Hungary in 1956 would not have been heeded, despite the clear American strategic superiority. The Soviet stake in Hungary was great if not vital; the American was not. For the same reason, *not* because of changes in the strategic balance, the Soviet leaders ignored repeated warnings from the United States not to intervene in Afghanistan in 1979, and not to build a base in Vietnam in the same year. Yet they did heed a private American warning in 1982 not to introduce MiG fighter-bombers into Nicaragua, because the stakes were recognized to be different. The United States could and did invade Grenada, and could invade Nicaragua today, without a crisis confrontation with the Soviet Union. (It should not do so, but for other reasons.)

In the Cuban missile crisis the American strategic nuclear superiority was overwhelming. I recall a three-star U.S. Air Force military planner saying with great confidence that we could destroy at least 90 percent, and possibly 100 percent, of the Soviet strategic nuclear forces before they could reach the United States. Yet the president was inclined against an air strike on the missiles in Cuba, among other reasons, because the U.S. Air Force could not guarantee even that all the missiles there would be destroyed. Even a surviving 10 percent of the small Soviet intercontinental striking force in 1962 could mean perhaps twenty or thirty American cities incinerated by thermonuclear weapons. The president did not want, in any case, to strike the Soviet Union, but in the crisis he was "deterred" in a sense by the possibility that matters would spiral out of control, and a nuclear war could mean millions of American casualties. That the United States could launch 3,000 strategic weapons against the Soviet Union and possibly be hit by only 30 (or at most a few dozen more than that) was no consolation. The mere possibility of nuclear war was the deterrent. While Khrushchev had a statistically much stronger reason for being determined to avoid nuclear war, his own thinking, and that of his successors under conditions of rough parity, strongly supports the conclusion that they, too, are determined that there must never be a nuclear war.

The global strategic balance is much less important in deterring or resolving crises than many have assumed, because the prospect of nuclear war deters even leaders who command an overwhelming superiority, as shown in 1962, and all the more so leaders on both sides with larger but more equal forces, as demonstrated ever since.

Similarly, as President Kennedy understood in 1962, particularly in dealings between the two nuclear powers, the side with greater power should not press its advantage too far. As Kennedy put it in his key speech at American University seven months later: "Above all, while defending our own vital interests, nuclear powers must avert those confrontations which bring an adversary to a choice of either a humiliating retreat or a nuclear war."[179]

Critics of the outcome of the crisis resolution usually argue that the United States could and should have "done better," driven a harder bargain. Specifically, they contend the United States should have been able to constrain further any Soviet military presence, and arms supply, to Cuba. I would argue that one lesson of the crisis is that it is important to do what you have committed yourself to doing, but a mistake to escalate demands. I think it was important to obtain the removal of the IL-28s because we had, from October 22, defined them as "offensive weapons." But I think it would have been a mistake, after the Soviets had accepted our central demands, to have suddenly raised new ones such as removal of all Soviet military personnel. Certainly with an eye to the future, it was important that the Soviet leaders understand that we always mean what we say; when we said "offensive weapons" we meant it—not less, but also not more.

An interesting question that has not been paid much attention is whether we should have *asked* for more in exchange for *giving* more. Restoring the *status quo ante* September 1962, removing the offensive arms from Cuba but leaving others, met our main interest. Part of that interest was to establish that the status quo should not

179. "Commencement Address at American University in Washington, June 10, 1963," *Public Papers: Kennedy, 1963*, p. 462.

be upset by a surreptitious unilateral Soviet military shift affecting the global U.S.-Soviet relationship. But the U.S. leadership did not really consider a more radical alternative: agreement to alter the status quo in a mutually acceptable way. A Brazilian proposal of October 25 may have offered such an alternative. The Brazilian proposal called basically for denuclearization of Latin America and a guarantee of the territorial integrity of all countries in the area. This would have involved, at a minimum, withdrawal of all Soviet nuclear systems from Cuba (and American ones from Guantánamo Bay and Puerto Rico), in exchange for no more than an implied renewal of commitments by all countries, including the United States, not to invade Cuba—and for Cuba not to invade any country in the region.

There were, however, also informal discussions of a possible broader deal under which the United States would have had to give up its base at Guantánamo Bay and return that territory to Cuba as part of a military neutralization of the island. The deal would have involved multilateral assurances against invasion of Cuba in exchange for a complete removal of both the Soviet and American military presence from the island, an end to external arms supply to Cuba, and Cuban nonalignment (still with its Communist government under Castro, but with a commitment not to join any military alliance or alignment).

If such an arrangement had been pursued, the United States would not have been acceding to any Soviet demand, but to a Latin American proposal. It would have had the broader effect of removing any Soviet military presence from the hemisphere. Though the United States would have given up something, it would also have gained much more than the status quo of September 1962. Moreover, and preferably, the deal could have been pursued *after* the resolution of the U.S.- USSR crisis on the same basis on which it was in fact ended. As a subsequent step, under Latin American initiative and auspices, the United States *and Cuba* could have entered into the agreement, with the Soviet Union an affected but only peripheral participant.

Under such an arrangement, the United States would have been able to seek a much more satisfactory relationship with Cuba.

Future Cuban military involvements in Angola and Ethiopia would have been avoided because the Cubans would not have had the necessary military establishment. And the United States would have benefited by disembarrassing itself earlier of its lingering covert operations against Cuba (whether as part of the deal, or through better recognition of its own interests vis-à-vis a militarily neutralized Cuba). Numerous frictions with the Soviet Union in the 1970s over constraints on allowed Soviet military activities in Cuba would also have been avoided. In the case of the 1979 Soviet brigade in Cuba, in particular, the cost of the episode in delaying and prejudicing the prospects for ratification of the SALT II Treaty may have been very high.

This brief excursion into an alternative outcome, if nothing more, suggests a connection between crisis resolution and broader political accommodation. That in turn raises the question of "preemptive" crisis resolution, or crisis avoidance, through political accommodation, a subject in which the Soviets have shown interest.

Crises, despite efforts to avoid them, do arise. And crises do involve a clash of aims and wills, and of the applications of power. One of the lessons drawn from the Cuban missile crisis by many of its participants and later analysts is the virtue of limited and graduated application of force. The quarantine, with the potential of being tightened, and with more direct military actions in reserve for possible use, worked. Perhaps it worked more as a tourniquet than as a step on an escalator, but it did stop a further buildup. Still, the quarantine by itself did not get the missiles removed; that took diplomacy and, as the Soviets stress, "mutual concessions."

It is not the Cuban missile crisis, though, that is usually seen as the test case for limited and graduated application of force. It is Vietnam. If, as many critics allege, the veterans of the missile crisis such as McNamara, Bundy, and Rostow later were tempted into an unsuccessful graduated escalation in the use of military power in Vietnam because of a lesson learned in October 1962, it was the wrong application of the lesson. I doubt, however, that the experience of the Cuban missile crisis had much to do with Vietnam policymaking.

What the Cuban missile crisis really demonstrated was that direct use of military force should not be resorted to when there are still diplomatic options for resolving a crisis satisfactorily. Military power may brace a diplomatic stand, and it may be required in some cases. But its direct use should not be one's first resort or resort of choice, if for no other reason than the inherent risks of losing control of the situation (and there are also other reasons). In the first days of the crisis deliberations in Washington, October 16 to 18, the case for an air strike seemed compelling to most members of the Ex Comm. Only on October 19–20, after many hours of discussion, did the disadvantages of that course and the feasibility of an alternative become the consensus judgment. And only after interaction with the Soviet leadership in the second week did the possibility of a mutually acceptable compromise become clear. For only then could a missile withdrawal for a noninvasion pledge be taken seriously, when it was learned that those were acceptable Soviet terms. Yet that deal was not even envisaged in the early Ex Comm deliberations.

This leads to another general conclusion: a crisis is an interaction, and it should be resolved through diplomatic interaction. Naturally it is necessary to clarify one's own priorities before entering a negotiation, but there should be sufficient flexibility in the positions one advances to allow movement in more than one direction, depending on the priority interests of the other side. It is sound to leave bargaining room, and to start well above one's "bottom line," but not to the extent of ruling out serious possibilities for negotiation by signaling a hard position on lines that may lead the other party to judge incorrectly that a line of interest to him has been ruled out. For example, an authoritative American statement in the first four days of the confrontation (October 22–25) suggesting a noninvasion pledge was absolutely out of the question might have cut off that productive line of negotiation. The United States did not advance a noninvasion pledge, not because it was unacceptable, but because its importance to the other side was not recognized at first. That was found only through diplomatic interaction.

Just as it is important in a crisis to determine the views of the adversary, so too is it useful in a consideration of the legacy and lessons of this crisis to seek and articulate not only American views, but also those of the Soviet adversary-partners in the experience.

For the Soviet view of the crisis experience, its significance, and its lessons, one must begin with the few key official statements made immediately after the event. Given the paucity of later Soviet information and analysis on the crisis, these early official explanations not only set the line for 1962–63 but provide the basis for the historical image of the crisis as understood in the Soviet Union for a quarter of a century.

Until October 28, 1962, the Soviet public record held that the United States had stirred up a crisis because of its designs on Cuba and denied that there were any Soviet missiles there. Then, suddenly, Khrushchev's letter of that date was published, setting forth the agreement to remove the missiles because of an American pledge not to invade the island. Next, on November 6, before the crisis was fully resolved, First Deputy Chairman of the Council of Ministers and senior Presidium member Kosygin commented on the situation in his leadership address on the anniversary of the revolution. Kosygin naturally stressed support for Cuba and blamed the crisis on "aggressive U.S. imperialism." He noted the U.S. president's pledge not to invade Cuba and to lift the blockade. "Now that, through compromise and mutual concessions, the conflict has lost its acuteness and talks are under way toward its complete liquidation," he said, "some people may ask: was it worthwhile to yield? In our view it was right to yield, for both sides, because this was a case of mutual concessions, of a reasonable compromise." He spoke also of "concessions on both sides, concessions to reason and peace."[180]

Kosygin had to acknowledge that there had been a major Soviet

180. "Forty-fifth Anniversary of the Great October Socialist Revolution, Report by Comrade A. N. Kosygin," *Pravda*, November 7, 1962.

Kosygin's very raising of the question "was it worthwhile to yield" strongly implies that some Soviet officials and citizens were asking that question. Soviet officials do not even rhetorically raise questions implying criticism or doubt as to the soundness of the leadership's decisions unless it is necessary to deal with them publicly.

concession, and it was natural and appropriate that he would put it in terms of "mutual concessions." Moreover, the Chinese had already sharply criticized Khrushchev and the Soviet leadership for "adventurism" in deploying the missiles in Cuba in the first place, and then "capitulationism" for taking them out. But Kosygin went further than a mere defense of the Soviet action as justified expedience. He reaffirmed, but also redefined, peaceful coexistence. "The Leninist policy of peaceful coexistence," he said, "implies admission by the two antagonistic systems on our planet, the socialist and the capitalist, that they live without war, that is, can coexist. This itself is a compromise, this itself is a mutual concession. It postulates that disputed issues will be settled not by war, but by negotiations based on the principle of peaceful coexistence, of peaceful competition."[181]

Khrushchev did not speak out on the crisis until he virtually had to do so at the meeting of the Supreme Soviet on December 12. (There is nothing in the publicly released record as to what he might have said at the Central Committee plenum meeting November 19–23.) The November 20 settlement of course had resulted in the raising of the American quarantine, but that occurred only in exchange for a further Soviet concession to remove the IL-28 bombers, while the basic American concession for the October 28 deal, a firm commitment not to invade Cuba, had still not been made. On December 12 that remained the situation, but Khrushchev could hold back no longer. He needed to make his case to the public.

Khrushchev's speech reiterated what was to become the standard explanation. "Our purpose was only the defense of Cuba," the missiles were placed in Cuba only to deter an American attack. And they had succeeded: "The attack on Cuba prepared by aggressive imperialist circles of the United States of America has been prevented." Further, "had there not been a threat of invasion . . . there would have been no need to place our missiles in Cuba."

181. Ibid.
This point was picked up at the time by the U.S. Embassy in Moscow; see telegram no. 1227, Moscow to State, November 7, 1962, p. 1 (Secret; now declassified).

He also attempted to bolster confidence in Soviet strength by stating there was no other reason to place missiles in Cuba, because the Soviet Union possessed "sufficient intercontinental missiles of the necessary range and power" on "our own territory."[182]

Khrushchev did not rest his case on the success of warding off an American invasion. He admitted that the Soviet leadership had "received information from Cuban comrades and from other sources on the morning of October 27 directly stating that this attack would be carried out in the next two or three days. We interpreted these cables as an extremely alarming warning signal. And the alarm was justified. Immediate action was necessary to prevent the attack on Cuba and to preserve peace. A message was sent to the U.S. president prompting a mutually acceptable solution."[183]

He stressed the need "to bring the negotiations to completion; to put the agreement on record," while also claiming that the U.S. president had already, "as the whole world knows," pledged not to invade Cuba. He said they were "pleased with the outcome."[184]

Khrushchev was on the defensive. He admitted that "some allege that the United States forced us to make concessions." But, he claimed, "if one employs such a standard, these persons should have said that the United States, too, was obliged to concede something." He also invited his audience to "imagine for a moment what might have happened had we acted like diehard politicians and refused to make mutual concessions. . . . If we had taken an uncompromising stand we would only have helped the 'lunatic' camp to use the situation to strike at Cuba and unleash a world war." But, fortunately, "among the ruling circles of the United States there are also persons who appraise the situation more soberly" and realize the futility of war.[185]

In sum, Khrushchev concluded that "a mutually acceptable

182. "The Present International Situation and the Foreign Policy of the Soviet Union, Report by Comrade N. S. Khrushchev at the Session of the U.S.S.R. Supreme Soviet, December 12, 1962," *Pravda*, December 13, 1962.

183. Ibid.

184. Ibid.

185. Ibid.

settlement was reached that signified a victory for reason." Who won? "Reason won, the cause of peace and of the security of nations won." He said that both sides "displayed a sober approach," and reiterating what Kosygin had said, "agreement was reached as a result of mutual concessions and compromise"; it was "a reasonable compromise."[186]

Soviet leaders rarely commented on the crisis in the months that followed, and Soviet historians have generally given it rather brief attention.

One other contemporary public statement should, however, be noted, and also a particularly interesting discussion appearing in a confidential journal. Both are especially significant because they concern the Soviet military.

Marshal Malinovsky, the minister of defense, published a booklet that happened to go to press just as the crisis broke. The manuscript had been submitted for publication on October 9, but it was not "signed to press" until November 28, permitting a brief passage to be inserted after the crisis was essentially resolved, although before Khrushchev's speech. As he had in his November 7 anniversary of the revolution parade speech, Malinovsky credited Khrushchev personally for his "wise proposals" that "showed the way to a reasonable compromise." Apart from these genuflections to the leader and to the official line, Malinovsky credited a "severe warning to the American aggressors and the taking of measures to increase [Soviet] combat readiness" as contributory. He did, however, also credit the fact that "the Soviet Union in those days exhibited a maximum of restraint and circumspection." Looking clearly with an eye to the interests of the military establishment, he said that "overcoming the crisis in the Caribbean is a great victory of the forces of peace. But it must not arouse a sense of complacency among us or dull our vigilance. . . . Our answer to any provocations of the imperialist aggressors must be the firmly established defense power of the Soviet Union, the constant combat readiness of its armed forces."[187] Malinovsky did

186. Ibid.

187. Marshal R. Ya. Malinovsky, *Bditel'no stoyat' na strazhe mira* (Vigilantly Stand Guard over the Peace) (Moscow: Voyenizdat, 1962), p. 14.

not speak about the withdrawal of the missiles, "mutual concessions," sober forces in the U.S. leadership, or new prospects for negotiation.

The other contemporary Soviet discussion also went to press before Khrushchev's speech laying down the official line. It is contained in an article by an unidentified civilian writing in the confidential General Staff organ *Military Thought*. Clearly, the Central Committee believed it important that an explanation and the line be given quickly, authoritatively, and confidentially to the leadership of the military establishment. Editorials on current foreign political situations in that journal are rare. In some ways, this article is the most interesting Soviet account of the crisis in all the literature. It has only recently become available in the United States, and is cited here for the first time.

The title of the article, "Be on Guard, Keep Your Powder Dry!" and its closing paragraphs are strikingly different from the rest of the article, enough so to suggest that they may have been additions of the military editors. The line they took was standard: "The brazen provocation of the United States against Cuba once again shows that we do not have the right in the slightest degree to weaken our vigilance, our combat readiness." And: "the Soviet Union unswervingly pursues a policy of peaceful coexistence of states with different social systems. But if the imperialists, despite the will of the peoples, unleash a new world war, they will receive a crushing retaliatory strike."[188]

Those are the concluding words of the article, but they are strangely irrelevant to its thrust and implied conclusions. The article begins by describing the crisis in the last ten days of October as "the most severe trial [for the world] since World War II." Matters, it seemed, "would reach a direct armed clash between the two most powerful world powers, the United States and the USSR, a clash that would inevitably have grown into a world

188. L. Sedin, "Be on Guard, Keep Your Powder Dry!" *Voyennaya mysl'* (Military Thought), no. 12 (December 1962) [issue signed to press November 21, 1962], p. 21.

It should be noted that while retaliation is said to be assured, there is no claim of victory.

thermonuclear war.'' The cause was simple: ''Aggressive actions of the United States against Cuba led to a most serious crisis in international relations.''[189] It is, by the way, the *only* Soviet discussion to refer throughout to the ''Cuban crisis''—the standard line of the ''Caribbean crisis'' had not yet been set.

The Soviet argument that the whole crisis emerged from long-standing aggressive American military designs on Cuba is made forcefully, not pro forma. The idea that a ''new situation'' had arisen in Cuba in mid-October (meaning, unstated, the American discovery of the Soviet missiles), catching the United States unawares, is strongly rebutted. ''An analysis of just the military dimension of American actions against the Cuban Republic permits no doubts that the Cuban crisis was prepared gradually, planned, like a long-thought-through operation is planned, and in no way was it a simple improvization.'' The article cited the immediate marshalling of forty-five warships and 20,000 soldiers, including 6,000–8,000 marines, and stated, ''Even with the modern equipment of the army and navy such a mobilization of forces cannot be accomplished in a few hours.''[190]

Finally, in that context, there is a very curious description of the American military reaction. ''Indeed, the spectacle of contemporary America, scattering its military bases all around the world, and at the same time quivering from fear over a handful of missile launchers which were installed in Cuba, created at least a strong impression. But it was clearly not a matter of a mood of panic in the Pentagon, although the American military in general didn't distinguish themselves by strong nerves. Cries of a Cuban 'threat' were sounded to cover preparation for an open aggression against Cuba. . . . A fear of Soviet missiles, although perhaps genuine, in this case served only as an excuse.''[191]

The article also has some observations, perhaps wishful or biased, reporting that the Latin American countries in practical terms gave only grudging support to the United States, and that in

189. Ibid., p. 16.
190. Ibid., p. 19. This refers to the long-planned U.S. Caribbean exercise.
191. Ibid., p. 17.

Western Europe "the unilateral actions of the United States [earlier-noted Defcon 3 alert measures], taken without concern for consultation with its partners on matters of life and death for some of them, will not facilitate growth in the popularity of the aggressive NATO bloc."[192]

While these observations on the American reaction (and other Western reactions) represent a curious explanation to be given to the Soviet military in 1962, the discussion of the resolution of the crisis, and its meaning for the future, are far more important in judging the legacy of the crisis in Soviet thinking.

Settlement of the crisis is described as a "reasonable compromise," resulting from "negotiations on the basis of mutual concessions," and "that outcome of the Cuban crisis cannot be evaluated other than as a victory for reason." Kosygin's statements on mutual concessions in his speech of November 6 are cited. The result is also described as "the only correct approach under the contemporary situation." Thus, the Soviet leaders (and the position taken is attributed to "the Soviet Government and Comrade N. S. Khrushchev personally") were said to have displayed "Leninist firmness and flexibility," and "cool, restrained, and statesmanlike wisdom."[193]

The American role in reaching a reasonable compromise with mutual concessions is mainly implied, but it is there. And there is a reference to "sound-thinking" Americans. "Sound-thinking elements in the whole world, including those in American society, draw from the Cuban crisis above all the conclusion that in our day no question in international affairs must be permitted to go to the brink of war." "The whole world" clearly includes the Soviet Union, although in the Soviet view the most likely source of carrying things to the brink is the United States. Hence a prime "capitalist" source is also cited as evidence. "Not by chance the influential organ of American big business, the journal *Business Week,* at the beginning of November has warned its government:

192. Ibid., p. 21. This was a hope.
193. Ibid., pp. 16–17.

'We must not give way to illusions that we can unilaterally repeat a balancing on the brink of war in the future.'"[194]

In terms of the impact on *Soviet* thinking the article declares that "a new, deep meaning has been given to the concept of 'peaceful coexistence of the two systems.'"[195]

Finally, the article includes a remarkable statement raising the question of a far-reaching basis for détente. "Will this crisis remain only an incident in the 'cold war,' or can it open a new and better page in the postwar history of international relations? There are serious grounds for putting the question that way."[196]

It is only by considering subsequent Soviet actions and reactions in international politics that one can weigh the practical impact of this early indication of what today in the Soviet Union is called "new thinking."

Most Soviet histories have given the crisis no more than brief mention. Dr. Anatoly Gromyko, son of the 1962 foreign minister, has written most of the more detailed Soviet accounts that appeared in the 1970s and early 1980s.[197] His accounts have benefited from access to the Soviet archives, as well as early published American accounts. They have presented a strong defense of the Soviet political and especially diplomatic handling of the crisis. His and all other Soviet accounts have, however, been limited by several factors. First, the Soviets continue to exhibit an understandable

194. Ibid., pp. 20–21.

195. Ibid., p. 21.

196. Ibid., p. 17.

197. See Anatoly A. Gromyko, "The Caribbean Crisis, Part 1: The U.S. Government's Preparation of the Caribbean Crisis," *Voprosy istorii* (Questions of History), no. 7 (July 1971), pp. 135–44; Gromyko, "The Caribbean Crisis, Part 2: Diplomatic Efforts of the U.S.S.R. to Eliminate the Crisis," *Voprosy istorii*, no. 8 (August 1971), pp. 121–29; Gromyko, *Vneshnaya politika SShA: uroki i deistvitel'nost', 60–70-e gody* (U.S. Foreign Policy: Lessons and Reality, the 1960s and 70s) (Moscow: Mezhdunarodnyye Otnosheniya, 1978), 301 pp.; Gromyko, *1036 dnei prezidenta Kennedi* (President Kennedy's 1036 Days) (Moscow: Politizdat, 1971), 279 pp.; Gromyko, "The Cuban Crisis," in *Mezhdunarodnyye konflikty* (International Conflicts) (Moscow: Mezhdunarodnyye Otnosheniya, 1972), pp. 70–95; Anatoly Gromyko and Andrei Kokoshin, *Bratya Kennedi* (The Kennedy Brothers) (Moscow: Mysl', 1985), 480 pp.

reserve about delving into the history of the whole affair because of a continuing sensitivity for Cuban reactions and Soviet-Cuban relations. Second, in addition to the usual Soviet reticence to address political and diplomatic decisionmaking by the leadership, there has also been a ban on such discussion involving Khrushchev; virtually all accounts written from 1965 to 1985 do not even cite his name. The most recent book, in 1986, does, and there is some opening up in the study of Soviet political history.[198] Third, the Soviets have not yet begun to publish accounts based on recently declassified U.S. records and renewed study. In time, however, they probably will, and they may even open up additional Soviet source materials.

The Soviet political scientist, commentator, and Communist party intellectual Fedor Burlatsky published a striking article on the crisis in November 1983, and a play based on it in 1986.[199] His account is a fictional pseudo-documentary on the *American* decisionmaking, based mainly on a Soviet interpretation of and extrapolation from the American literature. It is not very accurate as history, but that is not its primary purpose.

Burlatsky had several objectives in writing these pieces. One was a desire to capitalize on renewed interest in the Soviet Union in both the Kennedys and the Caribbean crisis.[200] But there were two more profound reasons. He wished to make the point, indirectly yet clearly, that it was both necessary and possible for the Soviets to deal with the United States, to negotiate and reach agreements, even in times of crisis. As Burlatsky has commented, it is dialectically possible to collaborate even when there are sharp tensions. At the time he wrote, in November 1983, there was a much stronger

198. Kokoshin and Rogov, *Serye kardinaly*, p. 350.

199. Fedor Burlatsky, "Black Saturday," *Literaturnaya gazeta* (Literary Gazette), November 23, 1983, pp. 9–10. It was reprinted in Fedor Burlatsky, *Voennyye igry* (War Games) (Moscow: Sovetskaya Rossiya, 1984), pp. 21–45. The play is called "Bremya reshenii" (The Burden of Decision), and it premiered in Moscow in February 1986.

200. A letter to the editor commenting on Burlatsky's article indicated that many Soviet citizens only now realized how dangerous the Caribbean crisis of 1962 really was! See A. Kurganov, in Fedor Burlatsky, "1984: What Does It Hold in Store for Mankind?" *Literaturnaya gazeta*, January 4, 1984, p. 15.

mood of tension and pessimism in Moscow than in the United States. (It was after the KAL 007 shootdown, the start of deployment of intermediate-range nuclear forces (INF) missiles in Europe, and the like.)

His second reason was an interest in crisis management. Burlatsky has concluded that it is important to realize that crises *can* be managed, if they occur; but it is also important to recognize that crises *may* not be managed, so they should not be permitted to occur. Burlatsky's lessons on crisis management, from studying the Caribbean crisis, are these: (1) close control over escalation; (2) direct communication between the leaders; (3) secret diplomacy; (4) readiness to compromise; and (5) never placing the adversary in a corner, always letting him have a line of withdrawal.[201]

From studying the Soviet literature, and still more from talking with many Soviet officials, diplomats, and academicians, I believe the Soviets drew some additional lessons from the missile crisis, particularly from their own experience. One was not to bluff. Another was not to challenge an adversary who is stronger, and its corollary, to become stronger oneself. But more broadly, I believe they drew the lesson that crisis avoidance was better than crisis management. Above all, political accommodation was possible, and preferable, from a basis of rough equality and on terms of rough equality. In any given case, perhaps in every given case, there may be greater advantages on one side or the other. But while that would carry some weight, the mutual desirability of maintaining stability in the relationship would tend to mean that most settlements would be on a basis reflecting the general equality.

As the Soviet leaders look back on the twenty-fifth anniversary of the missile crisis, I believe they have drawn general lessons along these lines. The anniversary is also being used for reassessment in the United States. Most encouraging, a conference in October of 1987, held under the very suitable and symbolically meaningful auspices of the John F. Kennedy School of Government at Harvard University, has for the first time brought some of the

201. My interpretation of Burlatsky's meaning and intentions has been greatly aided by two long discussions of these works with him.

key Soviet scholars on this subject together with their American counterparts and participants in the 1962 crisis. This welcome sign of a more open Soviet approach could contribute to a long-delayed effort to overcome one of the critical shortcomings of the situation in 1962 that precipitated the crisis: a disjunction in perceptions of reality. There must and can be a greater meeting of minds in interpreting reality, even though differences of interest will remain between the two powers which, in 1962 and today, hold the destiny of the world in thrall.

Both sides may already have learned that crises such as the one of October 1962 must be avoided. That none has occurred in the quarter century since that time suggests the lesson has been taken to heart. Nevertheless, the possibility of a crisis remains and so, too, does the need for both countries to continue to work toward assuring against any recurrence.

Memoranda from October–November 1962

Six memoranda written during the Cuban missile crisis and referred to in the text are reproduced in this Appendix to provide additional data. All were declassified with no deletions, with the exception of one reference to a diplomatic source in document E.

Document A

TOP SECRET [Declassified November 20, 1981]

MEMORANDUM   October 23, 1962

TO: S/P—Mr. [Walt W.] Rostow
FROM: G/PM—Raymond L. Garthoff
SUBJECT: Reflections on the Confrontation over Cuba

The Soviets have doubtless had a number of motives in establishing missile bases in Cuba. They have probably been tempted by the first opportunity to establish a counterpart to American bases encircling the Soviet Union. There can be little doubt that they have recognized that such an action is provocative to Washington, though they may have underestimated the compulsion to react vigorously.

The Soviet leaders probably calculate that the new period of tension (which, incidentally, they had sought in advance to moderate by their relatively quiescent stand of late on Berlin, Laos, and the like) can be exploited to their advantage. While there are several ways in which the United States could have reacted, and may still react, each would offer certain opportunities for Soviet maneuver.

From a period of exuberant confidence following the first Soviet *sputnik* and first ICBM test in late 1957, the Soviets have thrice marched up the hill on Berlin and down again. From a period of publicly anticipated and acknowledged Soviet superiority in over-all military power in 1960, the military balance has by late 1961 and since swung more and more against them, and above all this is publicly accepted. It may appear in Moscow that missile bases in Cuba represent both the first, and probably the last, opportunity to place a lever under the US positions of strength on the Eurasian periphery.

At the extreme, the United States might militarily neutralize Cuba, at a cost to the American posture of peace, but also at the price of impairing the image of the USSR as a global power. Since the United States has chosen to act in the first instance resolutely, but not drastically, both sides will have the opportunity of assessing world reactions to the limited measures undertaken.

The chief Soviet "strategic" assets are: an intercontinental capability which works to restrain the United States from sharp escalation; a powerful nuclear missile force poised against Western Europe; a quantitative advantage in conventional strength in Europe, and especially on the access routes to Berlin; a highly vulnerable situation in Laos; and now, the missile bases in Cuba. "Tactically" the Soviets have the advantages of: ability to match a selective blockade of Cuba by a comparable selective "filter" on Allied weapons allowed to go to Berlin; doubtless some sympathy for the view that "defensive" long-range missiles in Cuba are not essentially different from defensive long-range missiles in Turkey; the ability to trade off their Cuban bases for some inroads into the US overseas base system; and the "opportunity" to make the United States fire the first shot if they wish to precipitate an incident in the blockade.

The chief weaknesses in the Soviet position are: a basic military inferiority in the event of general war, compounded by Western alert and possible Western preemption in some cases; ineffective sea power either to challenge the American naval blockade, or to institute strictly reciprocal measures; and the inability to interpose their own power between that of the United States and Cuba at any acceptable risk.

These remarks are an incomplete draft of thoughts stemming from your request of this morning; being now fully engaged on more immediate aspects of the problem I am passing this on now without waiting for the chance to complete it, though I may return to it later.

cc: G   — Mr. Johnson
    S/AL — Mr. Thompson
    G/PM — Mr. Kitchen
    INR   — Mr. Hilsman

G/PM: R L Garthoff: pep

Document B

TOP SECRET [Declassified November 20, 1981]

MEMORANDUM   October 25, 1962

TO: S/P—Mr. Walt W. Rostow
FROM: G/PM—Raymond L. Garthoff
SUBJECT: Concern over the Course and Outcome of the Cuban Crisis

I am increasingly disturbed over indications that in all of our planning for the development of the Cuban crisis we have to our peril neglected one particular contingency: that the Soviets would react mildly and with great caution. A week ago we were concerned about strangulation of West Berlin, missile firings and exchanges of cities within the US and USSR, and other drastic and dangerous possibilities. Now the danger that looms large is not exchange of cities, but exchange of bases—at the extreme, the unhinging of our whole overseas base and alliance structure. It would be a remarkable thing if the Soviets were able to make substantial gains in achieving their main objective of weakening the alliances militarily and politically simply by exhibiting caution and indecision in the face of our initial stand. I can think of nothing that would more encourage the Soviets to create new Cubas and new distant military bases and local conflicts than would a net gain from their Cuban venture.

I am, as you know, in fullest accord with the objectives so resolutely outlined in the President's address. Yet I can not escape the conclusion that unintentionally we may be moving in a direction which in the eyes of Moscow, the American people, and history could make mockery of the statement that "further steps" may be necessary; it was presumed, of course, these would be further steps forward if they were necessary to achieve the objective of the "withdrawal or elimination" of the missile bases in Cuba. But a rush to find concessions that we can offer to achieve this objective could, to change the arithmetic in Lenin's phrase, mean "one step forward, two steps backward."

Negotiation is vastly to be preferred to direct military action, so long as it can achieve our objectives. That it is sometimes necessary to brace our diplomatic stand by resort to carefully considered military measures is, of course, manifest in the quarantine action itself. There are also still available means of increasing the pressure which we can bring to bear on the other side short of direct military action, in particular, broadening the blockade or commando raids on the missile bases. But any irresolution in enforcing the present quarantine, or in accepting a "freeze" on the present situation (thus closing off all options for intensifying pressure), or premature indications that we would "trade" other bases, would weaken greatly such strength as we now have to bring to bear in negotiation.

At the time of the President's address, and perhaps still today, the Soviet leaders have probably been quite uncertain as to whether the "initial step" was in fact only the first of a "one-two punch." Their caution to date has been a result of this uncertainty. But this is a wasting asset, if indeed not already a wasted one. When they realize the other shoe is not going to drop, they are likely to be emboldened in their actions and certain to raise their price in negotiations. If we seem to display a certain fear in our own actions, Soviet fear of these actions cannot fail to be lessened.

The terms for eventual negotiation might well include some give by the United States as well as by the USSR. But unless we are very careful, the business of letting the Soviets "save face" may come to involve losing our arm. The Soviets simply will not expect the United States to be offering concessions at a time when they have brought no counterpressure to bear on us in response to the quarantine. Any such indication (and the press is already rife with such rumors of trading off bases in Turkey, etc.) will mean to Moscow only that the United States is *not* prepared to *compel* the retraction of Soviet offensive power from the Western Hemisphere. One doesn't buy what is already his. If we concede that we must purchase the Soviet withdrawal, we undermine our right to compel it. The longer we haggle over terms, the more this is so. Moreover, the Soviets may be able to "sell" their missile bases in Cuba several times over. They can play us along on a deal exchanging Turkey for Cuba and then insist on broadening it out to include more and more United States bases—having already achieved most of their purpose simply by stimulating lack of confidence in the US alliance commitments. The missile bases in Turkey and Italy are not militarily important; this is, however, almost irrelevant. Berlin, too, is not *militarily* significant. The Turks and Italians have already shown alarm at unofficial indications of possible trade-off, and this alarm will both deepen and spread out to other areas, no matter how we seek to present the case in terms of suddenly acknowledged obsolescence and of renewed efforts to provide more modern long-range missile support from other locations and by multilateral agreements. There is a real danger that some of our Allies may believe that the United States is not only excessively concerned about the military threat to itself, but also that it is prepared to sacrifice some elements of its power and of its commitment to them in order to allay a selfish concern about a base near our shores.

I believe that the United States should make very clear that our objective remains the dismantling of present offensive bases in Cuba. We should emphasize our continuing readiness to discuss broader disarmament and other arrangements; and also our willingness to permit a United Nations presence to monitor the dismantling of existing offensive bases—but without raising the quarantine before the patient is cured. Discussions in a Summit meeting or other appropriate diplomatic interchange would almost certainly have to involve broad questions such as nuclear non-diffusion. However, it seems to me that we should approach such negotiations from a position of strength rather than a feeling of weakness. If we maintain the original resolve to use whatever means are necessary, though not more than are necessary, to effect the withdrawal of Soviet striking power from Cuba, I believe that the Soviets will in fact recognize that the United States does have the high cards.

cc: G   — Mr. Johnson
    G/PM — Mr. Kitchen

G/PM: RL Garthoff: pep

Document C

[For U. Alexis Johnson]
DEPARTMENT OF STATE
Deputy Undersecretary
G/PM

SECRET [Declassified November 20, 1981]

MEMORANDUM   October 27, 1962

SUBJECT: The Khrushchev Proposal for a Turkey-Cuba Tradeoff

Khrushchev now recognizes that his position is weak. The whole Soviet ploy with Cuban missile sites was probably based on a three-level course of action.

First, the Soviets hoped for, and probably expected, US acquiescence in the buildup of a Soviet missile complex in Cuba which would substantially augment Soviet strength in negotiations over Berlin, and in general. The appreciable military gain, while not seriously affecting the strategic military balance, could have been converted into a high card at the negotiation table.

Second, as a first-line fallback position, the Soviets could react to a US blockade or similar pressure short of direct military invasion or attack on the bases by proposing a trade of Turkish, Italian, and UK IRBMs for those in Cuba. It is the lower end of this range of action to which the Soviets have now fallen back.

Third, at worst, the Soviets would react to US military action against the bases by whatever forms of political protest were warranted by world reactions—even up to breaking diplomatic relations. The Khrushchev message of October 27 strengthens the conclusion that the USSR would not resort to direct military confrontation or reprisal—on the seas, in Cuba, or in Turkey. To date, the world reactions have not been what Moscow had hoped for; in particular, the unanimous OAS action must have been a severe disappointment.

The third course is still the remaining Soviet recourse if we reject their offer at the second level. The Soviet statement clearly evades any commitment to military action if the US should decline its offer and eliminate the missile site by unilateral military action. It states that the missiles in Cuba are in Soviet hands and would be used only if there were (a) an invasion of Cuba, or (b) an attack on the Soviet Union or any of her allies. It can scarcely be an oversight that the contingency of a strike to neutralize the missiles is not included in this commitment. The Soviets can probably still be compelled to withdraw the missile bases if they see the only alternative will be our destruction of them. However, even that outcome would almost certainly not provoke even limited Soviet military escalation.

The Turks have already made abundantly clear that they do not want to be compared with the Cubans, used as a pawn, or shorn of the Jupiters which have always been to them a proud symbol of their ability to strike back if they are hit. Hasty surfacing of long-held US military evaluations of the obsolescence of the Jupiters would be ineffective in meeting these strongly held views. The Jupiters are not important as a military-strategic asset—but, then, neither is Berlin. Yet both have elemental significance as symbols of the integrity of the Alliance and especially of our commitment to stand by the interests of each of its members.

The United States can, while solving the Cuban base question with determination, forcefully reaffirm its readiness to reach agreements on arms control and disarmament. We could thus indicate our pursuit of peace at the same time that we disposed of the latest Soviet disruption of the peace.

The United States has a unique opportunity to deal a major setback to the Soviet leaders, and once and for all to disabuse them—and others—of any illusion that the alternative to any Soviet gamble for high stakes will be not fallback advantages, but a defeat. Precisely such an outcome is the way to discourage such ventures in the future.

G/PM: RLGarthoff

Document D and Commentary

[For the Executive Committee of the National Security Council]

DEPARTMENT OF STATE
Deputy Under Secretary
G/PM

TOP SECRET [Declassified November 20, 1981]

MEMORANDUM   October 27, 1962

SUBJECT: The Military Significance of the Soviet Missile Bases in
           Cuba

1. The presence of 24 1,020 n.m. MRBM launchers and 12 or 16 2,200 n.m. IRBM launchers in Cuba provides a significant accretion to Soviet strategic capabilities for striking the continental United States. In view of the relatively limited numbers of Soviet operational ICBM launchers—at present an estimated 75—the missiles in the Caribbean will increase the first-strike missile salvo which the USSR could place on targets in the continental United States by over 40 percent.

2. At present, 20 of the 24 MRBM launchers are believed to be fully operational, and the remaining four will be within a few days. The first 4 IRBM launchers will probably reach emergency capability by November 15, and full operational status on December 1. The 8 other confirmed IRBM launchers will probably reach emergency capability by December 1, and be fully operational by December 15. An additional four IRBM launchers will probably be completed, but it is possible that the quarantine has stopped them. The current threat is thus 24 MRBMs; by December it will—unless construction is effectively stopped within a month—be augmented by at least 12 and up to 16 IRBMs. Each launcher is assumed to have the standard two missiles, allowing one reload (for refire in 4–6 hours). In at least one of the nine bases more missiles than launchers have been positively confirmed, and in general the number of identified MRBM missiles at least is sufficient to man all the launchers for an initial strike. Earth-covered bunkers suitable for storage or checkout of nuclear weapons are under rapid construction, and at least two of them now appear to be complete. There is one such bunker for each pair of launch sites.

3. The strategic significance of the Cuban missile complex is due not only to the substantial quantitative increase in megatons deliverable in a surprise first strike, but also by their effect on the US deterrent striking force. Approximately 40 percent of the SAC bomber force is now located

138

on air bases within range of Soviet MRBMs in Cuba, and almost all of it is in range of the IRBMs. If the present base complex in Cuba is completed late in 1962, and taking into account the estimated Soviet ICBM force for the end of 1962, a Soviet attack without warning could destroy an appreciably larger proportion of over-all United States strategic capability than it could if the Cuban complex were not included. The number of US *weapons* surviving and ready to retaliate on targets in the USSR would be decreased by about 30 percent, and would thus leave only about 15 percent of the number in our pre-attack force. This force could still cause considerable destruction in a US retaliatory strike, the Soviets could not rely on the degree of surprise assumed in the above calculation, and it is very unlikely that the Soviets would be tempted toward resort to war by the change in the military balance. Nonetheless, this represents a serious dilution of US strategic deterrent capability.

4. The reasons for the strategic significance of the Cuban bases are: (a) the size of the Soviet ICBM force does *not* allow coverage of SAC bomber bases and soft ICBM sites; the addition of the MRBM/IRBM force already on the island of Cuba *does* permit coverage of *all* such points, thus bringing under fire an *additional* 26 US ICBMs and over 100 B-47s; (b) the Cuban based missile systems have high reliability (80 percent), accuracy (1 to 1.5 n.m. CEP), and warhead yield (up to 3 megatons each for the MRBMs, and up to 5 megatons for the IRBMs); (c) the United States does not have BMEWS or other early warning radar on the southern approaches; and (d) as taken into account earlier, many SAC bomber bases are concentrated in the South and Midwest.

5. All of the discussion above is concerned with the missile complex now being completed in Cuba. There is no reason why the Soviets could not, if unimpeded by an effective quarantine, literally multiply the number of launchers to a force large enough to threaten the entire strategic balance of power. The Soviets have deployed over 500 MRBMs and IRBMs on their own territory, and the lesser cost compared to ICBMs would make a major expansion in Cuba very attractive.

Raymond L. Garthoff

Special Assistant for Soviet Bloc,
Office of Politico-Military Affairs

Commentary on Document D
A Retrospective Evaluation
of the Soviet Missiles in Cuba in 1962

It is clear in retrospect that the Soviet motivation for deploying medium-range missiles in Cuba did not arise from a belief that growing Soviet strength could be exploited, but from a perceived need to offset growing *American* strength and the prospect that it would outpace Soviet strategic growth over at least the following five years. In 1962 the American intelligence and policy community did not fully appreciate this fact because it tended to hedge uncertainty about future Soviet military programs by overestimating them; the Soviet leaders knew better. And the Soviet leaders, while probably also overestimating American programs, did not need to do so in order to see their own strategic position worsening. In one sense, the United States failed to anticipate the Soviet action in Cuba because it failed to recognize how desperate the Soviet plight seemed in Moscow.

One of the considerations in American decisions during the Cuban missile crisis in October 1962 was an evaluation of the military significance of the Soviet deployment in Cuba of medium- and intermediate-range ballistic missiles (MRBMs and IRBMs). It is well known that Secretary of Defense Robert McNamara said at the outset of the crisis that the military significance of the Soviet deployment was not unmanageable and could be offset without having to remove the missiles—whether by compelling Soviet withdrawal or, if that could not be done, by American military action. Not all agreed with that judgment, but the matter was quickly set aside because of President John F. Kennedy's assessment of the *political* consequences, both international and domestic, if the United States were to acquiesce in the Soviet deployment in Cuba. McNamara did not question that judgment, and he did not deny that there was military significance to the deployment. How the deployment would actually affect the military balance, therefore, did not become an issue of contention. Indeed, it was not even fully analyzed in the hectic week of initial decisions. But it remained a factor in subsequent decisions throughout the thirteen days of the confrontation until Khrushchev agreed to dismantle and remove the missile systems.

To this day in the voluminous published commentary on the Cuban missile crisis there has been little assessment of the *military* significance of the Soviet missiles. Many—although not all—analysts have discounted that factor far too much, not going beyond reference to McNamara's judgment or comments on the overall force levels of the two sides. It is, therefore, of interest to see a now declassified Top Secret analysis made at the climax of the crisis.

On October 26, 1962, I was asked to prepare for the Executive Committee of the National Security Council (Ex Comm) an analysis of the military significance of the Soviet missiles in Cuba. On the following day I submitted the requested memorandum, reproduced here as document D.[1] The information in that memorandum is substantially self-explanatory. Although none of the information in it was incorrect, subsequent additional information has modified the picture in a few respects.

First, the then-prevailing national intelligence estimate of seventy-five operational intercontinental ballistic missile (ICBM) launchers in the Soviet Union was high; in fact, the Soviet ICBM force at that time numbered forty-four operational launchers (plus six test and training launchers that could have been used in an emergency). This correction makes no essential difference, but it

---

1. I had been in constant touch with colleagues working on the crisis in the Pentagon and the Central Intelligence Agency and quickly prepared the brief analysis. My recollection is that I did not formally "clear" the memorandum with anyone (in those remarkable and heady days, it was possible to prepare such a memorandum and submit it to the Ex Comm within hours with no lateral "clearances"!), but that I did informally clear it with Harry Rowen, deputy assistant secretary, International Security Affairs (ISA), in the Department of Defense, and Roger Hilsman, director of the Bureau of Research and Intelligence (INR) in the Department of State. I did not clear the paper with the CIA because of time pressures, but the current intelligence on the status of the Soviet missile deployment in Cuba was provided by the CIA, as were the agreed intelligence data concerning Soviet strategic forces and the SS-4 and SS-5 systems and capabilities. The information on American deployments was provided by the ISA, based on an analysis prepared by William Kaufmann, a consultant to the ISA, and Robert Trinkle of Systems Analysis.

Table 1. *U.S. and Soviet Strategic Forces, October 31, 1962*

Weapon system	United States		Soviet Union	
ICBM launchers[a]	172	(+7)	44	(+6)
SLBM launchers[b]	112	(+32)	0	(+97)
MRBM and IRBM launchers[c]	. . .	(105)	. . .	(24 in Cuba)
Strategic bombers[d]	1,450	. . .	155	(+)
Warheads (salvo)[e]	±3,000	. . .	±250	. . .

a. The figures in parentheses are additional test and training launchers also available for use. The 44 operational Soviet ICBMs were all liquid-filled missiles requiring several hours of preparation for firing.

In mid-October in response to the crisis the United States began to expedite completion of Atlas and Titan ICBM launchers then under reconstruction. While this effort could not of course affect the American force level more than marginally during the crisis, it did raise the number of operational American ICBM launchers from 112 in early October to 210 by January 30, 1963: 126 Atlas, 54 Titan I, and 30 Minuteman I (this concluded the Atlas deployment; 54 additional Titan II launchers under construction were completed within a few months; the Minuteman I deployment continued until early 1967). Incidentally, this expedited, or "crash," deployment resulted in lowered quality standards and reduced reliability, although in any event the Atlas and Titan I forces were phased out within a few years. By contrast, the Soviet Union by January 1963 had still not quite reached the 75 ICBM launchers earlier estimated for mid-1962 and only reached about 100 by mid-1963.

b. The U.S. figures conservatively assume seven of the nine operational U.S. Navy Polaris submarines with 112 of the 144 missiles would have been immediately available. The 97 relatively short-range ballistic missiles on thirty-five Soviet diesel and nuclear submarines were all in Soviet waters and unavailable for early commitment, in addition to being highly vulnerable.

c. The 60 Thor missiles in Great Britain were subject to British control, and the 45 Jupiters in Italy (30) and Turkey (15) were similarly subject to Italian and Turkish assent. These 105 missiles were, therefore, not counted in the Strategic Air Command (SAC) order of battle, although they were conditionally available for the Single Integrated Operational Plan (SIOP). The United States did not seek to alert these forces, and indeed on October 27 President Kennedy instructed that the Jupiters in Turkey be kept nonoperational.

On October 28, the last of the 24 SS-4 launchers in Cuba was counted as "operational" by the United States, with the assumption that nuclear warheads were available, which they almost certainly were not.

d. Strategic bombers are here defined as heavy bombers or as medium bombers with basing and refueling support for intercontinental strikes.

The SAC ready-strike bomber force rose from 652 on October 19, 1962, to 1,436 on October 24 with Defense Condition (Defcon) 2, and 1,479 on November 4.

The Soviet Long Range Aviation force had a total inventory of 155 *Bison* and *Bear* heavy bombers, and a large number of *Badger* and *Bull* medium bombers. The bomber force was not, however, supported by tankers for air refueling, and even the heavy bombers were dependent on limited Arctic advance bases for round-trip missions against North America. The force did not go on high-readiness under the nominal Soviet alert.

e. The SAC bomber and ICBM ready force grew from 1,433 warheads on October 19 to a peak of 2,952 on November 4. To this must be added the U.S. Navy Polaris force with 144 warheads on nine submarines.

These figures do not indicate the substantial nuclear delivery capability of other U.S. forces: strike aircraft on the navy's carrier force and in the European and Far Eastern theater commands.

It is difficult to estimate the number of Soviet warheads that were available for a strike, since the forces were not alerted and the time to generate the force would undoubtedly have had to be limited. It could have varied from less than 100 to several hundred.

In both cases, the figures represent potential "salvo" force delivery in a *first* strike, with no account for missile refire or bomber restrike capabilities. Warhead stockpiles were much larger, at least in the case of the United States, and not the limiting factor in the Soviet case. Second-strike capabilities would have been reduced in the case of the United States, and severely reduced in the case of the Soviet Union.

reinforces the conclusion of the paper on the significance of the MRBMs and IRBMs in Cuba. Thus, completion of the deployment then under way, forty launchers, would in fact have increased the first-strike land-based missile salvo by 80 percent, rather than by 40 percent, from the lower base. In both cases, the ninety-seven Soviet short-range submarine-launched ballistic missiles (SLBMs) were not counted, because none was at that time deployed within range of the United States nor could they quickly have been brought here.

Critics might charge that even an increase that great in the Soviet first-strike missile salvo would not have altered the overall strategic balance. That, of course, was McNamara's point from the outset. As shown in table 1, the lineup (one cannot call it a "balance") of operational strategic forces at the end of October 1962 heavily favored the United States. Moreover, in quality the United States had a further lead (for example, all the Soviet SLBMs were short range and required surfacing of the submarine to fire, and two-thirds were on noisy, easily tracked diesel-powered submarines).

Nonetheless, the memorandum shows that the Soviet Union's move to increase its strategic capabilities by the Cuban deployment would in fact have posed "an appreciably heightened threat to the US strategic retaliatory forces" and hence to our deterrent capability. Thus a military concern existed in addition to the concern over Soviet intentions prompted by such a sudden and surreptitious gambit. Even if with hindsight these concerns can be considered excessive, they did not so appear at the time.

Second, the information in the memorandum represents the maximum extent of operational deployment before the resolution of the crisis on October 28.

Third, the United States did not know on October 27–28 the precise number of missiles in Cuba. We had identified thirty-three SS-4 missiles, but we knew that there might be more and that there might also be some SS-5 missiles. (Some supporting equipment unique to the SS-5 system had been identified, in addition to the distinctive SS-5 launchers.) In fact, the Soviet leaders then informed us that they had forty-two missiles in Cuba, and assisted us in observing the withdrawal of the forty-two missiles, all SS-

4s.[2] No SS-4s, SS-5s, or other MRBMs or IRBMs have ever been seen in Cuba in the twenty-five years since, and there is no reason to doubt that these forty-two missiles were the total number there. The deployment under way would have brought the number to forty-eight SS-4 missiles and thirty-two SS-5 missiles—providing the standard single reload for each of the forty launchers, as was correctly estimated. Delivery of the last six SS-4 missiles and all thirty-two SS-5 missiles to Cuba was stopped by the "quarantine" blockade; five of the Soviet ships then en route, which immediately stopped and soon returned to Soviet ports, were identified by intelligence analysts as probably carrying some or all of the SS-5 missiles and the remaining SS-4 missiles.

No nuclear warheads were ever identified in Cuba, but there was evidence that some were en route from the Soviet Union when the quarantine began and interdicted them. As noted in the memorandum, standard Soviet nuclear weapons storage facilities were built at the missile sites (one for each eight launchers).

The reference to the nine "bases" for missiles should better have read nine "groups" (of four launchers each). The fourth group of SS-5 IRBM launchers, the tenth group in all, was clearly planned and in fact construction work had been started, but had not yet proceeded far enough to meet the intelligence analysts' criteria as "confirmed"—hence the reference to "12 or 16" SS-5 launchers. All forty MRBM and IRBM launchers were located at four complexes or bases, each with its own Soviet ground combat team to provide local security.

In short, the assessment erred in assuming that some of the SS-5 missiles might already be in Cuba and in assuming that the nuclear warheads might be there. These were, however, the only prudent assumptions to have made under the circumstances.

Fourth, it is worth noting that in 1962 an accuracy of 1.0 to 1.5 nautical miles (for a very high yield missile payload) was considered good, and was indeed a threat to our early soft Atlas and Titan missile launchers and bomber bases, to say nothing of cities.

2. Some press reports at the time, mentioned in some later accounts, alleged that we had counted only thirty-seven outgoing missiles. These reports were incorrect and were based on the count on November 9, rather than the final count on November 10, when the last shipment departed.

Finally, if the crisis had ended with the United States conceding a Soviet right to unlimited deployment of missiles in Cuba, we would have entered a period of increased strategic instability. The United States would undoubtedly have replied with an augmented airborne bomber alert force and probably an even more rapid program for submarine missile deployment. If a compromise resolution had allowed some twenty-four to forty Soviet missile launchers to remain, but no more, the period of American strategic force vulnerability would have been much briefer than under unlimited deployment, though it is difficult to estimate the psychological effects both of the missile capability and of the American retreat to its acceptance.

One other comment should be made. Some revisionist analysts have implied or charged that in 1962 the administration intentionally cultivated a false impression that the missile launchers were imminently to become operational and thus required urgent and extreme steps. This charge is not well founded. As indicated in the memorandum, by October 27 twenty MRBM launchers were "believed to be fully operational" (by October 28 all twenty-four) and the even more threatening IRBMs were expected to reach emergency operational status in two weeks. We now know that there were no IRBM missiles yet in Cuba, and the SS-4 MRBMs probably lacked nuclear warheads, owing to the timing and effectiveness of the quarantine, but those facts were not known and could not prudently have been assumed at the time. Official concerns were genuine and were justified, even if they were erroneous; expressions of these concerns were not knowingly made alarmist.

This discussion has not addressed the question of whether American strategic superiority, or American conventional superiority in the Caribbean, was predominant in influencing the Soviet leadership to withdraw the missiles. I would not disagree with the judgment, affirmed by several of the principal decisionmakers at the time, that "the decisive military element in the resolution of the crisis was our clearly available and applicable superiority in conventional weapons within the area of the crisis."[3] Nevertheless,

3. Dean Rusk and others, "The Lessons of the Cuban Missile Crisis," *Time,*

the strategic balance undoubtedly did persuade the Soviet leaders not to counter in some other situation where they had decisive conventional superiority, such as Berlin. Both the strategic and conventional balances no doubt played a part. But even more decisive, in my judgment, was the balance of resolve, which also favored the United States. The Soviet leaders no doubt believed their action to have been justified, but they also knew they were taking the initiative in seeking to change the status quo. In that important sense they bore the responsibility for not permitting the situation to get out of hand as a result of any miscalculation of the American reaction.

For the American policymakers who dealt with the Cuban missile crisis in 1962, political considerations were dominant over military ones. Nevertheless, both political and military considerations reinforced their policy of resolve not to permit the deployment to remain.

September 27, 1982, p. 85; from a joint statement by former Secretary of State Dean Rusk, Secretary of Defense Robert McNamara, Undersecretary of State George W. Ball, Deputy Secretary of Defense Roswell L. Gilpatric, Special Counsel to the President Theodore Sorensen, and Special Assistant to the President for National Security Affairs McGeorge Bundy.

Document E

[For U. Alexis Johnson]

DEPARTMENT OF STATE

Deputy Undersecretary
G/PM

TOP SECRET [Declassified November 20, 1981]

MEMORANDUM   November 5, 1962

SUBJECT: Reprisals to Interference with US Aerial Surveillance

Unless we make crystal clear to the Soviets and to the Cubans that we will brook no interference with our unilateral aerial inspection, we will undermine any credence in our insistence on longer-range inspection in addition to making exceptionally difficult our own interim unilateral effort. If we are not prepared to take forceful steps to counter the use of force against ourselves, we will rightly or wrongly (and either would be bad) undermine belief that we would ever resort to force to meet intransigence on all the unresolved issues concerning present and future verification arrangements.

The Soviets have flatly said that all antiaircraft weapons were in Cuban hands [source reference deleted]. If it became necessary to undertake military action against Cuban air defenses as a result of their interference in our reconnaissance, we could make public the fact that the Soviets had informed us that such weapons were all in Cuban hands. This would reduce the already very remote possibility that the Soviets would react in any serious way to such actions on our part in reprisal.

Soviet military advisors and technicians were present with the Egyptian forces at the time of the Suez invasion in October 1956. We do not know whether any were killed in the Anglo-French strafing and bombing, but in any case the Soviets made no protest whatsoever. They did quietly evacuate their technicians through the Sudan as soon as that was practicable.

While it would be undesirable to undertake unnecessary military action endangering Soviet personnel, it would be even more undesirable to give them the impression that our resolve was so weak that we would permit Americans to be killed in conducting operations which even the Soviets have possibly recognized must now occur. Finally, as noted above, the

Soviets have authoritatively (whether correctly or—more likely—not) washed their hands of Cuban air defense weapons.

The best course of action would probably be to eliminate the interfering missile or gun sites or aircraft if possible, or comparable weapons on a reprisal basis.

G/PM: RLGarthoff: pep

Document F

[For Jeffrey C. Kitchen to U. Alexis Johnson]

G/PM

SECRET [Declassified June 10, 1977]

MEMORANDUM   October 29, 1962

SUBJECT: Significance of the Soviet Backdown for Future US Policy

1. Short-Run Effects

Political—The short-run effects should be very favorable to the US. Unquestionably the US will emerge from this confrontation with increased prestige world-wide. The Soviet action should demonstrate once again the offensive nature of Soviet motivations more clearly than anything we could say. It should also demonstrate that the Soviets are not prepared to risk a decisive military showdown with the US over issues involving the extension of Soviet power. (We should be clear however that this is not to be confused with Soviet lack of willingness to "go to the mat" over an interest vital to Soviet security.) More specifically, short-run political effects should include the following:

   a. Soviet ability to penetrate Latin America should suffer a reversal, though a base for future penetration may remain in Cuba for some time. Soviet intentions have been unmasked, and Soviet inability to force its will clearly demonstrated. Our problems in assisting Latin America to achieve a higher state of political and economic development will still require all of our best efforts. However, our efforts should be focused on the fundamental nature of the problem, and it is important that we continue to pursue our Latin American country internal programs, along with our broader development programs.

   b. NATO should be strengthened. The firmness of the US stand, and perhaps even more importantly the categorical refusal to barter NATO assets for immediate US security interests, should provide assurance of US commitment to the Alliance.

   c. Our position on Berlin should be greatly strengthened. Our resolute willingness to act in Cuba should result in a complete reassessment by the Soviets as to how far they can safely push US will in general, including Berlin. Similarly it should provide our Allies with fortitude for meeting Soviet threats.

   d. The effect upon the neutrals is more difficult to estimate, but in

149

general is favorable. It must raise in the minds of many of the neutrals who may have a pro-Communist leaning a question as to how far they may safely "get in bed" with the Soviets and still protect their own national interests.

e. While there is probably very little immediate effect on Soviet-Satellite relations, it cannot help but plant the seed of doubt as to Soviet omnipotence. This could have important implications for the future.

f. The effect on the USSR can be beneficial, but this will depend on how we further use our present strong position. It is conceivable that within the Soviet leadership the events of the past several days may be considered so serious a setback that changes may occur in the current Soviet leadership.

Military—The military benefits secured as a result of the Soviet backdown are similarly immense. Agreement not to proceed with additional missiles, and to dismantle existing missiles and launch facilities, cancels out the temporary increase in capability vis-à-vis the continental United States, which the Soviets achieved in their short-lived attempt to offset the current US nuclear strategic advantage.

2. Long-Run Effects

Political—An analysis of long-run effects is of course more uncertain. Unquestionably the Soviet defeat will have its impact on Soviet thinking and policymaking. Over the long run, one effect may be to make the Soviets far more responsive to our efforts at finding peaceful solutions to the whole range of world problems. However, and this is an important qualification, this effect is certain to take a considerable period of time. We should not delude ourselves into believing that great and rapid changes will result in Soviet policy. People and governments simply do not and cannot change that quickly, even assuming the stimulus for doing so. Thus while it is useful to explore all avenues of solutions to world problems, such as disarmament, we must not expect quick or easy solutions. We would expect that the US will meet with the usual Soviet criticism, resistance, and negotiatory pressure. In short, we must not slip into euphoria over the successful course of events, assuming it continues to develop favorably.

Military—Viewed in its long-run perspective, the Soviet backdown does not affect the Soviet military position in any important essential other than, of course, the important removal of the missiles from Cuba and awareness in Moscow of US refusal to permit *any* such venture. It is possible that the effect of these events might be to set in motion a redoubled Soviet effort to close the gap to development by the Soviets of a secure second strike capability.

3. General Conclusion

Our over-all preliminary conclusion may be summarized as follows:

a. We have in the recent situation gained broad political and military assets, on which we should attempt to capitalize. We have probably gained important, but less definitive, long-range benefits.

b. In these circumstances, it is vitally important that the US take the initiative in offering to negotiate on major issues between East and West. Without being bellicose in the basis of our new-found strength, nor on the other hand making concessions which would adversely affect our position of strength, we should press for fair but safeguarded solutions to outstanding problems.

If we have learned anything from this experience, it is that weakness, even only apparent weakness, invites Soviet transgression. At the same time, firmness in the last analysis will force the Soviets to back away from rash initiatives. We cannot now, nor can we in the future, accept Soviet protestations of "peaceful" coexistence at face value. The words may sound the same, but the meaning is different. Their willingness to cooperate in common endeavors can only be judged by performance. The difficult task for US policy in the future is to strike the correct fine balance between seeking cooperation from a forthcoming posture, while retaining the necessary strength and skepticism to insure ourselves and our friends against future duplicity.

RL Garthoff: pep

Index

Abel, Elie, 24n
Acheson, Dean, 29, 44n, 59n
Adenauer, Konrad, 73
Adzhubei, Aleksei, 46
Afghanistan, 113
Africa, Cuban forces in, 90n
Air reconnaissance: Soviet from Cuba, 102–03; U.S. over Cuba, 21, 23, 61–63, 68, 72, 99–100, 147–48
Air strike option, 30, 31n, 42, 53, 54, 58n, 59, 62, 71, 72, 112, 113
Alaska, 56
Alcatraz, Cay, 99
Aleksandrovsk, 75n
Alert, military, 3; U.S., 37, 38, 73, 109, 124, 132, 142n; USSR, 41, 73, 109; Warsaw Pact, 41, 73
Algeria, 21
Alikhanov, Artemy A., 64
Allison, Graham T., 9n
Alpha *66,* 16, 91
Alsop, Joseph, 27
American Embassy (Moscow), 39, 45, 58n, 119n
Anderson, Adm. George W., 58n
Anderson, Maj. Rudolf, Jr., 62
Angola, 116
Arctic, 142n
Atlantic Ocean, 21, 101, 102
Atlas (U.S. ICBM), 142n, 144
Austria, 12, 13

B-*47* (U.S. bomber), 37
B-*52* (U.S. bomber), 37
Badger (Soviet bomber), 142n
Bahia de Nipe, 101
Balance of power, strategic, 6, 9, 98, 112–14, 131, 139, 140, 145–46
Ball, George W., 19, 63, 67, 146n

Bartlett, Charles, 24n
Batista, Fulgencio, 90n
Bay of Pigs (*1961* invasion of Cuba), 3, 5, 10, 18n, 89, 90, 98
Bear (Soviet aircraft), 102–03, 142n
Berlin, and the missile crisis, 9, 26, 28, 33, 44, 112, 131, 132, 133, 134, 136, 139, 146; *1961* crisis, 41; post-*1962* crisis, 87, 88, 149; *1971* agreement, 88
Bernstein, Barton, J., 20n
Bison (Soviet bomber), 142n
"Black Saturday," 56
Blight, James G., 60n
Blockade, 12, 13, 16, 29, 49, 64, 71, 72, 118, 132, 133, 136. *See also* Quarantine, U.S. naval
Bluff, 54, 110, 127
BMEWS (Ballistic Missile Early-Warning System), 139
Bohlen, Charles E. ("Chip"), 28, 62, 87n
Bolshakov, Georgi N., 27, 28n, 111
Bombers: Soviet, in Cuba, 19n, 28n, 34, 66–74 (*see also* IL-*28*); Soviet strategic, 142; U.S. strategic, 138–39, 142 (*see also* U.S. Strategic Air Command)
Bowles, Chester, 27
Bratsk, 75n
Brazil, 45, 56, 115
Brezhnev, Leonid I., 41, 45, 101
"Brigade *2506,*" 89, 90n
Brown, Harold, 103
Brune, Lester, 23n
"Bugle Call," 45
Bulgaria, 6, 7n
Bull (Soviet bomber), 142n
Bundy, McGeorge, 19, 25, 38, 66, 70, 71, 72n, 78n, 89, 90, 116, 146n

153